"If leadership is more about who you a[re] in Flux is the perfect guidebook to keep [...] are becoming. Through relevant case studies, vivid sto[...] tical postures, and transformational prayers, you'll be equipped with what you need to keep being changed by Christ to change those around you."

Kara Powell, PhD, chief of leadership formation
at Fuller Theological Seminary and coauthor
of *Faith Beyond Youth Group*

"*Life in Flux* is a practical guide for tough times when it feels like we're stuck. Lisa and Michaela share stories, prompts, and practices to help readers develop skills for a more meaningful life. The book is useful for anyone but will especially resonate with those who find their purpose in Jesus Christ. I can't wait to get my physical copy as this book will be underlined, dog-eared, and frequently reread."

Cammie Dunaway, former chief marketing officer
at Duolingo, Nintendo, and Yahoo!

"Reading *Life in Flux* is like listening to a friend care for you with Ignatian sensitivity. Experienced, empathetic, practical, and trustworthy, Lisa and Michaela offer a path through transition that awakens the whole person."

Anne Snyder, editor-in-chief of *Comment* magazine

"This book is a life jacket, a compass, a sextant, and a steady voice of calm for anyone trying to navigate the storms of a life in flux. I am going to be assigning it to every one of my students and recommending it to every one of my clients. O'Donnell and Slayton have brought years of deeply attentive listening, wide-ranging scholarship, leadership experience, and their own authentic vulnerability to guide people through the most turbulent moments of life. You'll want to read, reread, and pass along the wisdom of this book to anyone in your life who is facing rough waters."

"In a whatever world, it is very difficult to know who we are, why we are, and therefore what we are to do. How would we ever know? And what difference could it make anyway? In their new book, Michaela O'Donnell and Lisa Pratt Slayton draw on years of unusually reflective and thoughtful experience with scores of people and places to offer windows into the integral relationship of ideas to life. Born of their unique ability to see and hear into the questions of honest people longing to make more sense of leadership, *Life in Flux* is the best of professional competence formed by theological maturity, rooted in every paragraph by hard-won wisdom about the nature of a True North and why it critically matters for individuals and institutions."

"*Life in Flux* is a balm for an ever-changing world where burnout is rampant. O'Donnell and Slayton are thoughtful, theologically grounded, and wise guides skillfully navigating through the ambiguity of liminal spaces and offering a praxis for transformation. As a loving leader and joyful disruptor at home in my own life in flux, my soul needs every compassionate, hopeful, and affirming word O'Donnell and Slayton generously offer as they guide us through the inner excavation, postures, and unfolding toward becoming integrated practitioners and flourishing leaders."

Life
in Flux

Also by Michaela O'Donnell

Make Work Matter

Life
in Flux

Navigational Skills
to Guide and Ground You
in an Ever-Changing World

MICHAELA O'DONNELL, PHD, AND LISA PRATT SLAYTON

BakerBooks

a division of Baker Publishing Group
Grand Rapids, Michigan

Published by Baker Books
a division of Baker Publishing Group
Grand Rapids, Michigan
BakerBooks.com

Printed in the United States of America

Library of Congress Cataloging-in-Publication Data
Names: O'Donnell, Michaela, 1983– author. | Slayton, Lisa Pratt, author.
Title: Life in flux : navigational skills to guide and ground you in an ever-changing world / Michaela O'Donnell, PhD, and Lisa Pratt Slayton.
Description: Grand Rapids, Michigan : Baker Books, a division of Baker Publishing Group, [2024] | Includes bibliographical references.
Identifiers: LCCN 2023050982 | ISBN 9781540901613 (paper) | ISBN 9781540903631 (casebound) | ISBN 9781493443321 (ebook)
Subjects: LCSH: Trust in God—Christianity. | Self-actualization (Psychology). | Social change.
Classification: LCC BV4637 .O36 2024 | DDC 248.4—dc23/eng/20240130
LC record available at https://lccn.loc.gov/2023050982

Some names and details have been changed to protect the privacy of the individuals involved.

Cover design by Laura Powell.

The authors are represented by WordServe Literary Group, www.wordserveliterary.com.

Baker Publishing Group publications use paper produced from sustainable forestry practices and postconsumer waste whenever possible.

24 25 26 27 28 29 30   7 6 5 4 3 2 1

For Evelyn and Sage.
May the sounds of home always guide you.
May you always know that you belong.
—Mom (Michaela)

For Roger.
My captain in the fog
for four decades and counting.
I love you.
—Lisa

No one ever steps in the same river twice, for it's not the same river and they are not the same person.

Heraclitus (author's translation)

CONTENTS

INTRODUCTION

I once heard a graduation speaker say something like, "To be a citizen of the modern world is to live a life of turbulence." Many experts agree, describing the current landscape in which we are living, breathing, and doing organizational life as volatile, uncertain, complex, and ambiguous.

Chances are you get it. You likely don't need to look very far to identify volatility at play in the world and, even more personally, in *your* world. Consider a housing market impacted by global supply chain issues or work-from-anywhere cultures that were accelerated by a global pandemic. If the last years have taught us anything, it's that no one escapes volatility in this world.

With that, the world is just *less certain*. There are many, many situations for which there are no longer clear or predictable answers. Consider the polarized nature of life in the United States. From guns to elections to climate change, the lack of collective certainty is everywhere.

In today's world, the issues that need the most attention are increasingly complex in that they are multifaceted and interconnected. The rise in global mental health needs, the changing nature of religious affiliation, even the evolving nature of how people use personal pronouns—these are complicated conversations, to say the least!

Add to all that the way our world feels ambiguous. There isn't usually just one path forward, is there? Sometimes it feels like there are four or five options, while other times it feels like there are none.

Yes, life today is in flux. Our lives and the world around us are subject to a near-constant flow of disruption and change. And honestly, that's a lot to take in.

For all the tough questions we run up against, let it be said that there are also so many bright spots—good people doing the work of cultivating skills for a life in flux. We see them firsthand! People who are navigating disruption in grounded and hope-filled ways. People who are meeting change with creativity and calm across life stages and industries. People who have seemingly learned how to navigate a life in constant motion.

That's what Lisa and I want for you too. To feel genuinely guided and grounded in a life in flux. To be at home even as things around you feel unfamiliar. To be secure as the world ebbs and flows.

Here, we've synthesized the culmination of our collective work— our accompaniment of thousands of people navigating flux, what we've studied, and the theological reflections that arose in response.

We've designed this book around what we are calling Navigational Skills for the inner work that helps each of us be at home in flux. Over the course of these pages, we'll move through eight Navigational Skills:

1. Wake up
2. Check your speed

3. Let go
4. Embrace the unfiguroutable
5. Set your compass
6. Come home to yourself
7. Don't go it alone
8. Stay in your headlights

While the skills are presented in a linear fashion, the work itself isn't linear. Sometimes it's not even logical. And while we're not claiming this is an exhaustive list, it's the most honest way we've seen people heed the invitation of God's loving grace amid disorientation.

When I was first drawn to write this book, I knew I didn't want to go at it alone. I wanted to work with someone who understood the ambiguity and complexity of the world as it is. Someone who had their own Navigational Skills and had spent years really helping people develop them. Enter Lisa Slayton, a trusted leadership coach and organizational consultant. Her ideas and frameworks are the fruit of twenty-five-plus years spent designing and facilitating spaces that catalyzed transformation with leaders. She knows what it's like to both live in flux herself and accompany others through it.

Though the book is in my voice for editorial reasons, Lisa's frameworks, stories, and words are with mine on every page. When we first agreed to write together, Lisa and I both came with our distinct frameworks—Lisa from her many years of coaching, consulting, and leading, and me from academic research, a cohort program I built that's helped hundreds of people navigate career transitions, and countless conversations I've had with people in flux around my first book. Early on in our writing process, it was clear that our readers (that's you!) would be best served if we fused our knowledge together and made space for something new to emerge. It was disorientating, to say the least, but the contents of this book are exponentially better than what either of us could have brought to you by ourselves.

This book is yours, meaning Lisa and I believe this book needs to be concretely useful to you. Toward that end, scattered throughout it are our favorite existing tools and written prayers to help you do the work of making your way forward in flux. We've also included signposts that signal shifts toward cultivating each Navigational Skill. In each, we draw a contrast between how we commonly posture ourselves and what the uncommon posture (the one that reflects cultivation of the Navigational Skill) looks like. Here is an example:

COMMON POSTURE: When the unexpected happens, I react.

UNCOMMON POSTURE: When the unexpected happens, I pause and reflect so that I can choose my response.

So, when you see these signposts, remember they can help you get a sense of your bearings about the work you've already done and about your sense of direction going forward.

Got all that?

Okay, then. Let's get started navigating our way through a life in flux.

1

Life in Flux

On a sunny Saturday morning off the coast of Maine, seventeen-year-old Roger Slayton set out on his seventeen-foot runabout with a handful of friends. Roger had spent every summer of his childhood in a small, coastal community where he'd learned the ways of the ocean. By this point, he'd been driving boats for years.

The problem? This was no ordinary day.

The boys spent the morning exploring different nooks and crannies on the coastline. After they had gotten good and far from the harbor, a thick blanket of fog suddenly rolled in. It was so dense that Roger couldn't see past an arm's length. He felt his heart start to race. He had lost all sense of where he was, and he knew it.

Before GPS and cell phones, the most important skill for anyone driving a boat was the ability to read charts. Like a road map, a chart tells you where all the waterways are, where they intersect with one another, and where the land masses are along the way. They indicate where you ought to be in a particular channel as you leave or return to harbor. Charts map the rock ledges on the coastline at low tide, out into the open sea, and around the islands. But when the fog rolls in, the charts are no longer useful.

The question becomes, If you can't see beyond your hand, how do you get your bearings?

That day, in the thick of the fog somewhere off the coast of Maine, what Roger did next might seem counterintuitive. Nonetheless, it was his only option. Lost in the fog, Roger decided to cut the engine of his boat and stay still in the water. Then he asked his friends to be quiet. He was listening, but for what?

Because the weather in Maine can be so unpredictable and change so rapidly, there is a set of navigational markers that are completely sound-based. These markers are never more important than when the fog rolls in. These were what Roger was listening for in the quiet that day. His ears were turned toward the sounds of the foghorns and bell buoys located all along the coastline, each having its own distinct sound, tone, and key based on which harbor it was marking. Roger was listening particularly for the sounds of his harbor, Ocean Point.

He was listening for the sounds of home. Because he knew that if he could hear home, he could make his way to it.

Even in the fog.

At that point, Roger was too far out to get back easily. Yes, he could recognize the Ocean Point foghorn, but he couldn't sort out how to get there. All he could do was take it one step at a time.

He started by trying to make his way toward any sound at all, knowing that, if nothing else, he could find the shoreline. On half a tank of gas, he didn't have much room for error. He had to be intentional about every single step. So, his rhythm became:

Stop.

Cut the engine.

Listen.

Take the next small step forward.

Repeat and course correct as needed.

As he started toward the sounds of the shore, he heard another boat ahead, so he pulled in close to ask for directions. It was a lobster boat that was anchored down and waiting out the fog too. When Roger and his friends asked the captain which way to Ocean Point, he lifted his hand and pointed, saying in typical Mainer fashion, "Thataway."

With just that bit of guidance, the boys set off in that direction, repeating the same process again and again and again.

Stop.

Cut the engine.

Listen.

Take the next small step forward.

Repeat and course correct as needed.

For many of us, the world feels a lot like this. We're less and less sure where to go or how to get there as the fog of life rolls in. While we're not literally out on the Atlantic Ocean, our world feels just as wild and uncontrollable as the open water. Things alter suddenly and intensely, often unexpectedly.

Then, we sense deep down that something has to change.

What got us to this point won't get us where we want to go next. Life is no longer linear or predictable; maybe it never was to begin with. On nearly every level of human life—ranging from giant, global realities like climate change to very personal problems like a job change or a health diagnosis—today's world is marked by disruption and disorientation.

One minute we can see the path in front of us, and the next, the fog has covered everything.

Dealing with Disruptions

People have long mused that the only thing constant in life is change itself. Today, more than ever, life feels like it's *in flux*—like it's in near-constant motion. This feels true on the thirty-thousand-foot level (Hello, globalization), on the ten-thousand-foot level (An aging workforce meets a distributed one, anyone?), on the thousand-foot level (Ugh, another season of drought in my state?), and on the ten-foot level (Oof, my friendships all feel different now that I'm in my forties).

Now, change isn't all bad. My husband and I moved with our children from the West Coast to the Midwest to be near family. While I miss the ocean, I have never once regretted watching my kids play with their grandparents. Lisa started her own consulting firm and loves the flexibility. I know teams of people who love that working from home is now an acceptable format, but at first it was a big change.

No matter the form, change is disruptive. It makes us feel all kinds of things, and the more sudden, prolonged, ambivalent, or complex the change feels, the harder it is to move through. This is true even for the changes we are happy about—a new baby, a big promotion, a new relationship. Though we're thrilled with change like this, it still messes with our sense of settled. It disrupts the way we've learned to make sense of the world. It forces new rhythms and takes a toll on our relationships.

And when disruption stacks on top of disruption? It's, well, a lot. Consider the man who moves to a new city for a new job during an election year and then loses a parent right before Christmas. Or the woman who starts her own business so she can work from home in March, only to have her husband get laid off in June, find a lump on her breast in July, and have her kid transition to middle school in August.

It's no wonder life feels like a fog.

It's no wonder we feel disoriented.

Though many types of disruption leave us feeling foggy, *transitions* have a way of making us feel particularly unsure about where we're headed. Transitions are any type of event in which we move from one thing to the next, usually through a period of disorientation and stress.[1] My work over the last several years has put me up close with many people in the midst of transition, usually related to their work. People looking to make a career change or who have been laid off. Those who are feeling the pangs of a new structure at work or who have just launched out on their own. Those who are returning to the workforce after time away or who are managing new employees.

On the topic of transitions, author Bruce Feiler's work is helpful. In *Life Is in the Transitions*, he reports that in the West, people undergo significant transitions every twelve to eighteen months, which means most people experience thirty to forty major disruptions in adulthood.[2] A promotion, moving a parent, moving into a new place, a change in religious beliefs, changing schools—the list goes on. If you're nodding in agreement here, know that you're in good company. But, wow, that's quite a bit of the seas of change for us to bear!

On top of that, Feiler's research shows that people undergo more dramatic transitions three to five times in a lifetime, on average. Getting married, retiring, the death of a spouse—he calls these *lifequakes* and defines them as "a forceful burst of change in one's life that leads to a period of upheaval, transition, and renewal."[3] The shake-up with these kinds of transitions is often much more intense.

Transitions can be either personal or collective, voluntary or involuntary. These in-between spaces happen to us sometimes as individuals and other times collectively, sometimes by our own volition and sometimes not. For example, if you are fired from a job, that's a personal and involuntary transition. If your church decides to plant a new church, that's voluntary and collective. A recession is involuntary and collective. Getting married is voluntary and personal.[4]

So, based on Feiler's findings, we can expect to experience a meaningful disruption every twelve to eighteen months and a really big disruption a handful of times throughout our lives.

Now, add the things that happen to the people closest to us but aren't exactly happening to us. Your sister wants to make a career pivot, or your spouse goes to work at a new firm. Your best friend becomes the primary caregiver for her mom. You feel the ripple effects of those disruptions, right? They aren't happening directly to you, but you might carry their stress all the same.

We live our lives in a series of systems. This means that an action in one part of a family, organization, or society impacts the other parts of that same family, organization, or society.[5] If Dad loses his job, parents might fight more or the kids' grades might go down at school. If lumber is hard to come by, homes don't get built and prices might skyrocket. If more people work from home, we have to reimagine the purpose of office buildings.

Fog is everywhere.

On nearly every level of society, the systems we rely on are growing more destabilized every day. Our health care system, our workplaces, our ecological environment, our cities, our schools . . . in all these spheres, our existence is set against the backdrop of and intimately interwoven with the reality that, almost anywhere we look, things are changing in complex and accelerating ways.

Disruption, both personally and collectively, is not a new phenomenon. What is new is the speed at which the world is changing and the rate at which we go through major transitions in our own lives. The pace of change almost feels exponential.[6] Today, we see the results of accelerated change all around us— the hurry of weekly life, ever-changing demands at our jobs, and the digital nature of, well, almost everything. There are, of course, upsides to disruption, but most of the time it just feels like there are a thousand choices to be made and no time to make them.

As humans, we used to have more time to catch up to big changes. Take technology, for example. A thousand years ago, technology developed much more gradually. Experts say it took about a hundred years for an innovation to have a widespread impact on people's everyday lives.[7] When something like the printing press was developed, people had a generation or two to catch up to the invention—to really grasp and feel its impact.

However, the world started to speed up around 1900.[8] As it did so, the time we had to adjust to the impact of technology shortened. When innovations like the light bulb, the automobile, and the telephone came onto the scene, their widespread impact was felt in as soon as thirty years, shortening the period of adaptation by seventy years!

Today, the time it takes innovation to impact everyday life is even shorter: only seven years.[9] The issue? Our brains cannot handle this pace. It typically takes the brain about ten years to adjust to these types of changes. So, while humans are adapting to change faster, it's still not fast enough to keep up. Technology is outpacing us. It's too taxing, too demanding, too disorienting. We literally cannot cope. Our brains are not made to accomplish that many things at once.[10]

What are we supposed to do? How do we find our way out of the fog that disrupts our daily lives? The temptation is to try to keep up, busy ourselves, or try to move forward quickly. It's natural, as soon as we realize we're disoriented, to press hard for clarity so we can feel sure about where we're headed.

This is when reality hits. What got us to where we are won't get us to where we want to go. Trying to go harder or faster only leaves us lost and exhausted.

It doesn't get us any closer to making our way in the fog.

We're Taking on Water

Choppy seas can almost always be felt at the spot where a river funnels into the ocean. That's where being able to read the waves is essential. The goal is always to keep the nose of the boat up so that the waves don't come over the sides, leaving the boat swamped.

In other words, you want to avoid taking on water.

When my son was two months old, my best friend showed up on my doorstep. She was getting a divorce. My husband, two kids, and I lived in a two-bedroom house with one tiny bathroom. We had a newborn who didn't sleep and ate every few hours. It wasn't a great time for a houseguest, but she was my best friend.[11]

So, she moved in.

By day, I'd do the things one does to keep a baby alive. By night, I'd listen to my friend talk about all that was unraveling in her world. Our ritual was to chase spoonfuls of chocolate chip cookie dough with sips of beer. (Yes, cookie dough and beer. You're welcome.)

After several days of this arrangement, I was beyond spent. Trading precious stints of sleep for stories of pain interlaced with bites of cookie dough wasn't exactly working. I called my mom, who is my person in these kinds of moments. She said something to me that I've shared with thousands of people since.

"Michaela, you're like a little boat. And you're taking on water. Unless you intentionally let the water off the boat, you're going to drown."

By the sheer fact that we are citizens of modern life, we all have a tendency to take on water. We eat dinner against the backdrop that war has broken out somewhere in the world. We drop our kids off at school only to fear in the back of our minds for their safety. We go to sleep at night worried about the disparate demands we don't have enough time for that await us the next day. We carry with us the weight of trying to attend to our world while taking in what's happening all around us.

These are rough, high seas we're in here. If the waves feel relentless, it's because they are. Soon enough, we're taking on a lot of water. It is all just too much for our beings to hold. Like my mother said, unless we intentionally let water off the boat, we're going to drown.

Let's be clear: It's not you. You're not the problem here. It's not that you're not strong enough, or evolved enough, or faithful enough. No, it's that the world is too much. The fog is too thick. The seas are too choppy. Your boat was never intended for this much chaos.

How can we know we're about to go under?

It might be that we've put our heads down and are powering through, making intentional choices to ignore the needs of our minds and bodies. (Hello, guilty!) Or we might slowly retreat emotionally, checking the boxes of life but not much more. These are all indicators we've taken on too much. When we're healthy, our systems can self-regulate and keep us in the zone between calm and alert. But as we become overwhelmed and unsure about what to do next, we end up feeling all sorts of things—confused, helpless, sad, even despairing. Those feelings? They're signs we're taking on more water than our boats can hold. They're signs we're deep in the fog. They're signs we're trying to make our way out.

What do we do? When we're unsure of how to move forward, it's easy to revert to old ways of being.[12] Because life in flux requires us to make our way without the kind of clarity that most of us would prefer, it's natural to double down on whatever has gotten us to where we are. It's natural to put our heads down and just keep going. But this sense of *keep going* is literally killing us. In our frenetic efforts, we've taken on too much water. And, like Roger, we have only so much gas. We have to make our way wisely and thoughtfully toward shore, and we won't make it by impulsively heading into the waves.

Instead, we'll make it by taking it one step at a time.

From Here to There

When the clouds of chaos loom in multiple directions, it's as if nowhere feels stable or safe. We might not have a good sense of what direction we want to go at all! In order to get our bearings and chart a new course, the first thing we have to do is really understand where we are and where we hope to go.

We have to name *here* and have (even a murky) sense for *there*.

For Roger, *here* was out at sea, and *there* was safely docked in his home harbor. For you, the answer will obviously be different. Though you will have any number of personal *heres* and *theres*, there's a big collective one Lisa and I want you to consider. We find a cue in the apostle Paul's letter to the Philippians. Eugene Peterson's translation captures the sentiment nicely:

> I've learned by now to be quite content whatever my circum-
> stances. I'm just as happy with little as with much, with much as
> with little. I've found the recipe for being happy whether full or
> hungry, hands full or hands empty. Whatever I have, wherever
> I am, I can make it through anything in the One who makes me
> who I am. I don't mean that your help didn't mean a lot to me—it
> did. It was a beautiful thing that you came alongside me in my
> troubles. (Phil. 4:12–13 MSG)

Here's the thing: Because life in flux is here to stay, our goal is to be at home in the One who makes us who we are, no matter what happens. So, if *here* is overwhelmed and depleted by disruption, *there* is feeling content no matter what happens.

It is tempting to think of getting there as strategic work—good action plans and skill building. But make no mistake, the Navigational Skills we need to make our way in flux have to do with *inner work*—the work we undertake over time to become more wholly the people we're uniquely intended to be. Doing our inner work includes growing in our capacity to face our shadow side, letting go of the masks and protectors we wear, and becoming deeply grounded and at home in God and with ourselves.

It's a process of waking up, letting go, getting to really know ourselves, and discerning what is ours to do. It takes time and practice to develop this kind of internal navigational system, and it requires us to check our assumptions and learn new ways of being. There are no tips and tricks to move quickly through hard work.

Several years ago, I became increasingly curious about what it would take to create a holding environment that helped others do inner work in the midst of transitions. Toward this end, my team at the Max De Pree Center for Leadership at Fuller Seminary and I designed, iterated, and facilitated a cohort experience that creates space to navigate pain, name longings, and take risks in the midst of seasons of professional transition.[13] To date, a team of a dozen wholehearted guides has accompanied hundreds of people through these cohorts.

All kinds of folks show up to these cohorts. People who want to make a career change. Those who *need* to make a career change. Some have bad bosses. Others want to go back to school. Some have had change happen abruptly or unjustly to them. Others are entering a new season of life on their own accord. Many come because of a professional reason but end up focusing on more personal stuff.

Everyone is in flux.

Pair this with the in-depth, often long-term coaching Lisa does with individuals and organizations that gives her a front-row seat to just how turbulent modern life feels. From this, we've observed some markers of what it looks like when people start to adopt new Navigational Skills. These are the ways many of us tend to shift.

1. From panic to pause.

Sometimes panic sets in. Whether we're triggered or overwhelmed, our ability to think clearly seems to evaporate. We either freeze, fight, or flee. This is normal brain function; in fact, it's core to our survival. If we perceive a threat, we panic and react. But reactivity isn't a sustaining tool. It won't help us move forward to where we really want to go. Popularized by Stephen Covey, and referencing Austrian psychiatrist and Holocaust survivor Viktor Frankl, there's an unattributed quote that gets at this quite well: "Between stimulus and response lies a space. In that space lies our freedom and power to choose a response. In our response lies our growth and our happiness."[14] Not only do we have agency in how we respond but even our most patterned responses can change. We can choose how we respond, and we don't have to choose panic.

Back on the boat, Roger may have had an initial panic reaction when the fog rolled in. Ultimately, he stopped and paused to choose a different response. With a half tank of gas, he knew that panic would not get him home. His friends were not experienced out on the water. In fact, they may not have realized the gravity of the mess they were in. They had to rely on Roger, and, fortunately, he had the inner skills needed to navigate forward. But accessing these skills in a stressful moment required him to pause rather than panic.

As we begin to do this inner work, we have to learn to recognize what sends us into a panic. In this, it can be incredibly helpful to work with a therapist, coach, or spiritual director to reflect on situations, types of people, and words that might trigger us. If a professional feels hard to access, we can do some of this work with a mature mentor or friend. As we do this work of reflection, we're inevitably transported back to traumatic events or past relationships that we may not have worked through yet, so care and a safe environment, which a professional or loved one helps to create, are key. Over time, in asking these hard questions, we learn more about who we are and how we want to interact with disruption. From there, we can prepare to shift from panic to pause.

2. From anxiety to anticipation.

Anxiety is not always bad. It helps us assess threats and notice opportunities. Of course, if we suffer from debilitating anxiety, it is important to address its real and devastating impacts with medical and therapeutic interventions. Outside of this, we know that some level of anxiety can be a motivating energy force in our lives if we can learn to recognize it as such. According to the American Psychological Association, it's different from *stress* in that stress is our body's reaction to a threat; it triggers the initial fight or flight response and usually comes from an external source, like a deadline, a family emergency, or a new situation. *Anxiety* is our body's response to stress and comes internally as we continue to worry and have symptoms even when the external stressor is no longer present.[15] The symptoms for each can look similar—insomnia, irritability, fatigue, muscle pain—so getting a proper diagnosis if they persist is of vital importance.[16]

Anxiety and stress, when present at certain levels, can create the kind of discomfort that is actually required for us to grow and learn. Physicians and therapists sometimes use what's called the *stress continuum* to quickly evaluate a patient and assess what kind of care they need. The continuum is usually color coded and ranges from healthy/positive (green), to reacting (yellow), to injured (orange), to ill (red). Green indicates optimal functioning, adaptive growth, and overall wellness. Yellow indicates mild distress, always goes away, and is low risk. Orange is persistent distress, leaves an emotional scar, and is higher risk. Red is the danger zone of persistent and ongoing distress, mental illness, and evidence of unhealed trauma. Green and yellow are most often manageable within our own support systems; orange and red require professional support and intervention.[17] It's important to note that the stories, skills, and tools shared here assume you're operating in the green or yellow zone and can thus harness normal levels of anxiety for growth.

Of course, we all love feeling calm, right? We want to freeze-frame life on the patio chilling with friends or the quiet moments after an easy day at work. While those are great moments, they aren't growth moments. It's not until we take on a stretch assignment, are pressed up against a deadline, or have to have a challenging conversation with someone we love that we actually can learn and grow from the press of stress and anxiety.

We can shift from anxiety to *anticipation* when we come to befriend the stress that emerges in disruption and helps us forecast where we might grow. When we start to reframe our anxiety in this way, it begins to evoke real expectation and even excitement as we move toward a learning opportunity. Of course, this doesn't mean that every tough thing that happens ought to be reframed as positive, or that we should skip over deep worry. Stress and worry are a natural and ongoing part of life in flux, and we have to know how not to push past the feelings we'd rather not feel.

3. From distraction to presence.

Every day we have so many stimuli coming at us that it seems impossible to be anything other than completely overwhelmed, preoccupied, and distracted. We engage in virtual calls while checking email and responding to texts. We scroll social media while helping our kids with homework and making dinner. Being busy and multitasking are the hallmarks of modern life. In fact, it is these stimuli and distractions that often produce the anxiety we just named.

Think about how you start and end your day. Consider how you fill your in-between moments. Do you run outside for a minute to listen to the birds? Do you pause to feel the fibers of the blanket between your fingers? Or do you check your inbox and scroll on your phone? Do you "optimize" your day, working to fit one, two, or ten more things in?

When the fog rolls in, we have to be attentive and attuned in order to make our way forward. We cannot cultivate that attentiveness and attunement in those disorienting moments; these postures must already be woven into the fabric of our lives. We have to choose to eliminate distraction as best we can in order to remain present to the moment we're in.

4. From fear to courage.

The poet David Whyte writes, "To be courageous is to stay close to the way we are made. . . . The first courageous step may be firmly into complete bewilderment and a fine state of not knowing."[18]

When transition happens or when change is brewing (especially when our own transformation is impending), it often creates real fear. This is true in our circumstances but also in our hearts and minds. As a change or disruption is in motion, it becomes hard to know what to do and how to think. The Navigational Skills we've spent a lifetime honing simply don't work, and that's when fear can creep in.

Afraid, Roger and his friends could have just randomly set off in a direction, hollering for help in hopes that someone might hear them in the fog. But reactivity is neither sustainable nor productive.

Making our way through disruption requires a tiny but monumentally courageous first step: going deeper into the fog. See, courage rarely comes from within. It is not muscled up with willpower alone. More often, someone who cares about us or whom we encounter on the journey urges or prompts us to be courageous. Roger had been equipped and encouraged by a community of more seasoned boaters over a number of years, so he knew that giving in to fear would not help him get safely home.

Other times, like with the Old Testament figure Joshua, the call to courage comes straight from God, who loves us dearly, beckons us forward, and promises to be with us wherever we go.[19] God's love is our True North and, thus, the source of our courage for the way forward. Turning to God is the first (and likely best) step to move from fear to courage.

5. From knowledge to wisdom.

Proverbs 4:6 tells us: "Do not forsake [wisdom], and she will keep you; love her, and she will guard you" (NRSVUE).

We live in an age of information. It's almost as if the sheer vastness of input we have access to forces us to assume our job is to acquire more knowledge. How often have you sat across the lunch table from someone who asks a question about something, and without even skipping a beat, you pick up your phone and google it, quickly finding thousands of bits of information about that thing? Now you have lots of information, which, if you choose to study a bit more, can become knowledge.

The verse above suggests that getting wisdom will cost us "all we have." Oof. When we remember it's true that wisdom grows most deeply out of our own suffering and pain, that can make the journey worth it. A child touches a hot fireplace and burns their little fingers, even after being told multiple times that it could hurt them. Does it hurt? Yes. Did it cost something? Definitely! But a burn like that will likely keep them safe next time.

The world is full of competent experts on any topic we can imagine, but much fewer who are wise. Uli Chi, author of *The Wise Leader*, describes wisdom as hospitable and gracious, an expression of love, and, ultimately, empowering of the other.[20] If knowledge is about what we acquire, wisdom is about what we give away. The work of making our way when disorientation sets in inevitably requires some knowledge, but it's wisdom that will propel us toward where we need to go.

How will you know when you have started to make these shifts? That you're cultivating Navigational Skills that will help you deal with disorientation and help others do the same? It takes a lot of reflection and self-assessment and a lot of hearing from others. A lot of stopping to cut the engine and really listen. It doesn't happen quickly or all at once. The work isn't linear. Honestly, it's hard, internal, deal-with-your-stuff work. It's develop-new-ways-of-being-and-thinking work. Not everyone wants to do it, but those who do will find themselves moving forward, step-by-step, out of the fog.

The Paradox of Growth

We've already said that it's tempting to think that the way we get from here to there is by trying harder. That in order to develop a navigational system for the fog, we'll need to do more strategic, practical work. The problem is that this would be a technical solution to an adaptive problem.

See, leadership scholars distinguish between two kinds of challenges: *technical* and *adaptive*. Technical challenges are ones for which there are known answers—making budget cuts to lower costs, taking medication to reduce inflammation, going through training to learn a new job. Even if these challenges are difficult or complicated, there are known solutions that can be found within ordered systems.

Adaptive challenges, on the other hand, require us to wrestle with our own deeply held assumptions and values. Developing new products for an industry in peril, transitioning to a healthier lifestyle to lower stress, learning how to regulate stress and set boundaries in a toxic work environment—these are all circumstances that require us to try something new. When it comes to adaptive challenges, there is always inner work involved. Adaptive challenges require value and mindset shifts. These shifts require waking up, letting go, embracing the unknown, and getting to know who we are deep down inside, all at a pace and scope that are fruitful. Adaptive challenges require us to move into a place of curiosity—a place where the systems are complex and the problems have no obvious root cause.

The work of building a navigational system suited for seasons of disorientation is adaptive work. At the heart of it are unlearning and dealing with pain. It takes deep work to attune more clearly to God's love as True North.

> **COMMON POSTURE:** Give me the steps to navigate change. I'll just follow the plan.
>
> **UNCOMMON POSTURE:** Help me embrace the long, slow work of becoming that will help me be at peace even when life is in flux.

So, how do we actually do it? How do we grow? How do we become more alert to God's voice as we make our way through life's disorienting seasons? The way forward is paradoxical in every way.

The way down is up.
We have to look back to go forward.
If we want to go far, we must go together.
We have to slow down to make progress.

Different teachers talk about this paradox in different ways, including the celebrated teacher Fr. Richard Rohr. In *Falling Upward*, he draws on the seminal work of psychologist Carl Jung to articulate a vision for two distinct quests in our lives. The first quest (not marked by any specific time stamp) is to build a *container* for our lives. We figure out what we're going to do for work and who our people are going to be, and we focus on learning about what makes us significant. In a sense, this first journey is one of *ascent*. The second quest is about deepening the *contents* of that container. We ask different questions. We get in touch with our fragility and pain in different ways. We uncover the true self found in Christ. This part of our journey is a *descent*, which taps into the reality that we must go down to come up.[21]

One of the most vivid illustrations of this paradox of growth is found in the metamorphosis of a caterpillar into a butterfly. If you study this amazing process, you will learn that once the caterpillar has done its job of eating and growing, it appears to intuitively know that it is time for the chrysalis to be formed. You've likely seen them hanging from a branch in a little J-shaped package. More recently, scientists have gained new insight into what exactly is happening in the chrysalis. Using MRI technology, they've discovered a caterpillar has very little in its makeup that indicates it will become a butterfly.[22] The two kinds of cells that make up the caterpillar are called imaginal and larval cells. Once the chrysalis is formed, the transformation begins as the imaginal cells consume and digest the larval cells to form some of the structures and systems that will ultimately become the adult butterfly.

What emerges from the chrysalis is a radically transformed insect that exists very differently in this world. The caterpillar exists solely to eat and grow. That's its job. The adult butterfly exists both to pollinate and perpetuate very specific flowers and plants and also to reproduce.

In short, growth has happened. A new way of being has emerged.[23]

We navigate a life in flux by being willing to grow, and growth helps us anticipate that the fog will come. Deep contentment trusts that the fog is a place of transformation.

There is a theological concept that captures the kind of hope that believes in both what's out there and also what's right here. It's called the *now and not yet*, and it is language that frames the Christian belief that the kingdom of God is simultaneously a here-and-now reality and an eternal phenomenon. If ever there were a theology that helped us frame the near-constant liminality that accompanies life in flux, this is it.

To become disconnected from the here and now in pursuit of the someday is ironically shortsighted. In contrast, to be so wrapped up in reacting or over-functioning in any given moment signals that we might be missing the bigger picture of all that is to come.

But it is not common to be adept at holding the now and not yet. To posture ourselves in this way is to trade any misdirected allure about what might be for the reality that is and the hope of what will be.

This includes our willingness to be present to suffering. This doesn't have to be bad news though! If we look for the Christ who is *already suffering* with his people and courageously allow that suffering to speak to the person we are becoming—to frame our understanding of what God is doing—then we find more of God in it. In 1989, celebrated author Henri Nouwen made the case that

> The leader of the future will be the one who dares to claim [their] irrelevance in the contemporary world as a divine vocation that allows him or her to enter into a deep solidarity with the anguish underlying all the glitter of success and to bring the light of Jesus there.[24]

The future is now, and tomorrow is just around the corner. The liminal air we breathe is here to stay. If we take Nouwen seriously, then it's likely that, in our world of constant demand, it is lasting contentment, focused attention, and genuine service that will lead us toward deeply coherent lives—but such lives will also come at the cost of our own relevance, spectacularness, and power.[25]

This is the path of discipleship—the counterintuitive journey of what it means to follow Jesus. Talking to his disciples, Jesus describes how the leaders of the times lorded their authority over people. "Not so with you," he says to his followers. "Instead, whoever wants to become great among you must be your servant" (Matt. 20:26). Yes, the paradoxical way of Jesus is that we have to go down to go up.

The same is true for us today. When we find ourselves in the throes of one of life's many changes, paradox is often central to the way forward. Just like with caterpillars, things usually have to get messy before they get clear.

That day on the coast of Maine, Roger had left home without the most important navigational tool a boater needs: a compass. The only way he was able to make his way home was with the development of a kind of inner compass. He had honed the skills to slow down, attune, move slowly, and course correct.

That day, Roger and his friends made a pact. They would all work together to determine which direction the sounds were coming from. This meant that if they didn't agree, they had to pause a little longer and listen a second time. Roger knew the sounds of home, but he couldn't make his way there alone. At last, the boys began to see a hazy line of white rocks emerging in front of them. Roger noticed familiar landmarks, which helped him really get his bearings. But as tempting as it was to go straight for land, he knew that they should not get too close because of the rocky ledges that might be just under the water's surface.

Just one small crossing away from their home harbor now, Roger kept the slow and measured pace that had guided them this far. Home was in sight.

A Prayer for When
I'm Lost in the Fog

Lord, the sky is hazy and the air is thick.
I can't see beyond my own hand.

I don't quite know how I got here.
I have no idea which way to go next.

But I've also been here before.
My anxiety follows me around.
I react before I've taken a breath.

And yet I do not know this place.
Where am I, Lord?
Where are you?

When I'm unsure,
I trust that
you go before me.
You are for me.
You are behind me
and within me.

And for that I say amen.

Do not leave me out in the fog.
Stay with me and guide my way forward.

Amen.

Prepare
to Wake Up

As Sarah opened the door to the fluorescent-lit building, she paused under the weathered awning for a moment. Her cheeks were wet with tears. Even as the taste of salt washed over her lips, she knew her only option was to go inside. She had to keep moving. So, she did. She walked by a handful of her coworkers, eyes focused on her phone as she tried not to signal that anything was wrong. She headed straight for her desk, flipped open her laptop, and squared her shoulders to her inbox. She ignored the lump in her throat and told herself to just get lost in emails.

Head down.

Don't look up.

Sarah had just been yelled at by her boss—again. The previous six months had been anything but calm. When she was hired, Sarah was given a very specific set of goals that she was well suited to accomplish. But when she tried to actually do that work, her boss would sweep in at the last minute and undo it all. While he told her that he wanted things to change, his actions showed otherwise. He cheered her on in public but minimized her in private conversations. She was confused, discouraged, and increasingly angry. The worst part was that she had several people who reported to her, which meant that their work was being undone and blocked as well. Before long, her boss's micromanagement and her subsequent unhappiness poisoned the entire team.

As she reached the end of what she felt like she had to offer, Sarah realized she needed to make a change. This was years before the work-from-anywhere boom, and she was living in a small college town. She needed a new job in the area, and she feared her search could take a long time. She started to look for new jobs, and a mentor encouraged her to also focus on the one thing she could actually control *now*: herself. No matter what she did next, it would benefit her soul to change the way she reacted now. Without taking on the onus of the blame for her toxic work environment, there were still ways she could grow.

But that growth would require her to wake up to all that was really happening. To open her eyes to see the layers of systemic inequity and her own enabling tendencies. To recognize the company's shifting priorities and what seemed like a revolving door of people leaving. To acknowledge, worst of all, the way what was happening at work was putting her on edge at home. She'd have to face the stuff that's sometimes hard to name, or see, or even believe.

The fog had settled in, and under its cover, Sarah was waking up to the fact that she had absolutely no idea what to do. She took her mentor's advice seriously. She believed it would benefit everyone if she could change the way she reacted. If she could somehow feel grounded in the midst of so much dysfunction and uncertainty. If she could wake up and find a new way forward.

NAVIGATIONAL SKILL #1:

Wake Up

I recognize that life is in flux, and so I realize what got me to where I am won't get me to where I want to go.

Something happens—whether suddenly or over time—where we literally wake up to the fact that we don't know how to go forward. Sometimes it's subtle, but often, it's dramatic. Waking up is, on the one hand, clarity (*I can't do this anymore!*) and on the other hand, deeper fog (*I don't know what to do!*).

It might sound kind of odd to talk about *waking up* as a skill. After all, it's something our bodies do every day without prompting from us. What's interesting is that experts suggest infants have to learn to fall asleep because the skill doesn't come naturally. (Hello, my children!) Parents go through somewhat extraordinary efforts to help their babies learn this skill (ahem, also me). So, as babies we must learn to fall asleep, and as adults we must learn to wake up (remember that growth paradox?).

Of course, I don't mean waking up from a good night's sleep here. Instead, I'm talking about waking up to all that's happening in and around us. Opening our eyes to all that we may have blinders on to or that we've pushed away because it's just too hard to see. Looking at the stuff that leaves us disoriented. Acknowledging the circumstances and challenges that settle in like fog.

Pain and Possibility

Though all kinds of disruptive events can usher in seasons of waking up, Lisa and I have observed two common catalysts: *pain* and *possibility*.

Let's start with pain.

Ugh, I know.

I recently met my friend Caroline for coffee. As she sat down, I noticed the way her coffee sparkled in the sun, but her face appeared heavy. She had just changed jobs, so I asked her how her new role was going. Exhaling deeply, she told me that the tech company she worked for was about to lay off thousands of people, many of whom she predicted would be in her department.

That day, Caroline was in the fog.

I immediately felt heavy with sadness, thinking about all the lives that were about to be disrupted—all the pain and anxiety that surely lay ahead. But when I asked Caroline if she was anxious, she said no. She told me in no uncertain terms that while this was a difficult moment, one in which she might even lose her job, she was not afraid. Her posture felt uncommon to me. When I said as much, she told me the painful story of how, about a decade earlier, her life had completely fallen apart. She'd gotten a divorce, moved to a different city, and done a major career pivot all within a two-year period. The life she knew was turned completely upside down as big, hard discoveries got stacked on top of other big, hard discoveries. Secrets surfaced and relationships ended; Caroline felt like she had been launched violently out of a cannon only to find herself suspended in slow motion in midair. Realizing that she didn't know what or even whom she could trust, she wasn't even sure she could trust herself. All the habits, practices, and postures she'd relied on to live, cope, and grow as a person felt completely useless in the slow-motion free fall she was in at the time.

This was Caroline's waking-up period. In fact, that's exactly how she described it to me over coffee that day. (Yes, she used the same language we do!) What had she woken up to? The fact that not everything was as it seemed in her life. The reality that only by leaning in to her grief would she ever be free from its hold.

It's worth saying that, as a society, we don't embrace going deeper into our grief. We often push it away and cope with our pain in other ways. So, when it comes time to do this work, not only are we ill-equipped but we lack models to do it well. Psychotherapist and author Miriam Greenspan adds weight to this claim by describing that we go through somewhat extraordinary efforts to avoid the emotions we as an American society deem as negative—feelings such as grief, fear, and despair.[1]

> **COMMON POSTURE:** I try to avoid pain—grief, fear, despair— at all costs.
>
> **UNCOMMON POSTURE:** I prepare, knowing that pain and dark emotions are inevitable and are valuable teachers.

Shortly after Pixar released the movie *Inside Out*, our neighbors and their five-year-old son stopped over. Seeing a promotional poster I'd gotten from the movie, the boy became really excited, having just seen the film himself. I was working on setting out some snacks, and I mindlessly offered back what I assumed was a developmentally appropriate comment.

"Yeah, wasn't Joy great?" I commented. "What a great main character!"

"Well, actually, Ms. Michaela, it was Sadness who saved the day," the young boy pointed out.

Besides the fact that he was obviously a bright and emotionally complex child, he was also right in his interpretation of the movie's plot. The breakthrough in the movie happened when Sadness was elevated to center stage and deemed the one who could give the protagonist, Riley, the space to deal with the loss she was experiencing. What's more, the perpetually optimistic and hopeful Joy came to realize that, when fused with Sadness, the two could come together as one to encapsulate all those blurry seasons of life that are neither solely joyful nor solely sad but both at the same time.

So much of learning to wake up is becoming aware of what we would rather not see—what feels safer to avoid than deal with head-on. Like me diminishing the role of Sadness in the film, we are taught to diminish the emotions within us that are deemed negative. And thus it becomes counterintuitive not only to deal with pain but to prepare for it to take center stage. We know it will cost us something. We know it will be hard. We know deep in our gut that waking up will take us places we do not want to go. It will move us toward the work of grief, lament, and unanswerable questions.

Still, we must choose to wake up.

Caroline wasn't afraid of the hard feelings that came with so many layoffs. She wasn't held back by the fear of losing her own job. She knew that God had guided her through the fog before; she trusted God to do the same again. She had cultivated the skills to attune to God's voice in disruption. She had come by them honestly, after all.

Pain is a powerful disrupter, but so is possibility. Waking up can also happen when a new possibility emerges. Sometimes, what's ahead is new enough that we sense we'll have to evolve and grow as people in order to fully embrace it. Then, life in flux feels a little more exciting, doesn't it?

Take Stacey, for example. She was a rising star at her accounting firm. She valued both margin and mission, which meant that both the partners and clients loved her. Plus, she was reliable— always willing to go the extra mile to help a colleague or take on complex situations. Naturally, as the partners in the firm started to think about long-term succession planning, they hoped Stacey would want the promotion to partner.

For her part, Stacey was terrified. She intuitively knew that even though she was an excellent accountant, she didn't yet have the skills to be a partner. It was a different level of responsibility and leadership than she'd had in the past. Stacey didn't like doing things she wasn't good at or didn't have a plan for; it was this very temperament that made her such a good accountant. But her reliance on the skills she'd worked so hard to hone, along with her natural wiring and personality? It was standing in the way of her future growth. Trying to picture herself in the role caused too much disorientation. And because she had not yet invested in Navigational Skills that could help her deal with that disorientation, Stacey ended up turning down the opportunity.

From the moment she said no, she wondered if she had made a big mistake. A few months later, one of the senior partners at the firm offered to help her make a plan for growth that would ready her for such an opportunity in the future. Excitedly, Stacey took him up on the offer. The firm invested in a coach for her, and it was in that context, with the promotion off the table, that she got to unpack some of why it was so important for her to exercise a sense of control over her environment. After six months with the coach, Stacey had a breakthrough. She was finally waking up to what she wanted deep down inside: she wanted to be a partner, even though she was anxious about it. It was only after this acknowledgment that she could become willing to accept something others had already embraced: the only way for her to learn to be a partner was by actually doing it.

In this, Stacey was subjecting herself to a state of disorientation for an unknown amount of time. The risk of failure was there. The promise of feeling inadequate was high. But the possibility of being engaged in work she loved in an increasingly meaningful way—a way that might directly impact a rising generation of accountants and a roster of clients whom she loved—was worth enduring the fog.

COMMON POSTURE: I stay with what is known and comfortable because the risk of failure is unacceptable.

UNCOMMON POSTURE: I open myself to possibility, knowing that the only path from here to there requires me to take risks and that failure is an opportunity for growth.

In both pain and possibility, small course corrections can make a big difference. For boats crossing the Atlantic, a half degree might be the difference between landing in Iceland or in England. We will all have small moments of waking up; there are much larger opportunities to come. Part of the work of waking up is recognizing these moments and opportunities for what they are. It's easy to stay in our comfort zones and not want to risk making a mistake or failing. But in doing so, we miss the potential for growth and flourishing, both our own and that of others around us.

Sometimes Waking Up Is Collective

When I was eighteen, my dad and I flew to visit a college in Ohio. Our route meant that we had a layover in the Twin Cities. As we stepped off the plane in Minneapolis, we were greeted by a pair of soldiers carrying weapons so large that I ducked behind my dad. As I followed in his wake through the airport, there were at least a dozen similar pairs of soldiers throughout, all outfitted for war.

It was early October 2001—just weeks after two planes crashed into the Twin Towers in New York City on September 11. Even as a kid, I understood that everything had become different then. Different if you were going to fly, different if you were Muslim, different if you were in the armed forces, different if you lived in New York City—just like that, life was different for us all.

There are certain events that shake the collective status quo. World events like 9/11, World War II, or the first moon landing. The invention of the automobile, the computer, or the internet. The tragic loss of household names like Martin Luther King Jr., John F. Kennedy, or Princess Diana.

The boom of smartphones and social media. The 2008 housing crash.

Tragedies like Columbine, Parkland, and Pulse Nightclub. Deaths like Ahmaud Arbery, Breonna Taylor, and George Floyd.

In the spring of 2020, we were thrust headfirst into a series of massive, worldwide, collective wake-up moments. You likely remember where you were and what was happening when you heard the news that life as we knew it was going to be paused because of something called a coronavirus. For a while, we expected it to be just that—a pause. How could the world not resolve itself and get back to normal?

Think back on all the conversations you had in those early months of 2020 that started with, "When things get back to normal . . ." This collective assumption revealed much about what we hoped would be true. But to me, it also revealed a collective truth for navigating a life in flux: how hard it is to wake up to the reality that the only way forward is by embracing something new.

We did not want to shelter in place or stand in line for toilet paper. We did not want our kids to do kindergarten or senior year over Zoom. We did not want to get sick or to say goodbye to loved ones over the phone.

It was all just too much.

We were overwhelmed, bewildered, and discouraged. Collectively, we were waking up to the truth that, deep down, we longed for something different. In so many areas of life, the pandemic awoke that which lay latent beneath the surface, bringing on major shifts in how we thought about things like where we lived and what we did for work.

In that season, everything was in flux.

Amid all this, people were coming to terms with the fact that, maybe, we weren't actually hoping for normal after all. Maybe what we wanted instead was space to process and make sense of all that was happening—space to pause, step back, and put words and feelings to what we were experiencing. Space to call attention to that which had been broken all along.

In this, the layers of collective and individual waking up were intertwined. In this, our hope turned toward the reality that the best way forward required something new. In this, we would have to get in touch with whatever it was we wanted deep down inside.

Longing for Home

When the fog rolls in, we all typically find ourselves wanting one thing: home.

Yes, we all long to make our way home. Of course, I recognize this can get complicated, depending on our experience of home. If our childhood home was unsafe, or life in flux means we've lived in twenty-seven different houses, longing for home may feel counterintuitive or abstract. Still, I think there's something in us that longs for the security, comfort, and permanency of whatever we perceive home to be.

Because we've observed how much people long for home, Lisa and I read widely on the topic. We've also asked dozens of ordinary people two questions:

- How do you define home?
- When do you most long for home?

Their answers were both instructive and breathtaking. One favorite reply came from a first-grade teacher who said, "Home is a place where you don't have to think about being yourself. You don't have to impress anyone. It's where you are the most comfortable, where you feel loved the most. You long for home when you are feeling inadequate or uncomfortable. You long for it when you're down."

She's right. Home is where we are known, safe, and loved. Where we don't have to pretend to be anything other than ourselves. Sometimes home is physical. Other times it's not. Sometimes we're born into a sense of home. Other times we have to create it from scratch and fight for it every step of the way. There can even be a sense that home still eludes us. .

In his instantly classic memoir, *Surrender*, legendary rock icon Bono reflects on his own reckoning with pain this way. He writes, "We were beginning to understand how complex is the search for home, especially if you have pain hiding there. And that the small things are often the big things."[2] As we set out, we anticipate both sorrow and joy. And we trust that in looking honestly at the small things, we are taking on the big things too.

While we're deep in the fog of life, of course we long to feel settled—with ourselves, with each other, and, perhaps most deeply, with God. The more uncomfortable or stretched we are, the deeper the longing becomes. When we're out at sea, tossed around by the waves and engulfed in a blanket of fog, it might feel overly simple to say that the work is mostly about learning to hear the sounds of home. Trust me, though, this first step is anything but simple.

The good news of the story of God is that we all have a home in God. One that's rich with love, grace, and acceptance. Because of that, we can sing with the psalmist: "Lord, through all the generations you have been our home! Before the mountains were born, before you gave birth to the earth and the world, from beginning to end, you are God" (Ps. 90:1–2 NLT). Jesus himself puts it this way: "Remain in me, as I also remain in you" (John 15:4). In other words, "Make your home in me as I make my home in you."

An amazing thing happens when, as Henri Nouwen says, "We realize that right where we are, right here in this body, with this face, with these hands, with this heart, we are the place where God can dwell."[3] We are the home of God, just as God is our home.

In a world in which we sometimes feel the need to be everything and do everything—to believe that more is always better—God's promise that we have a home in Jesus based on nothing other than the fact that we are known and loved is a deep sigh of relief.

Yes, our sense of home in God is not earned or fickle. The story of the prodigal son shows us as much. It holds one of the most tender portrayals of God's welcome for us, as an aging father rushes to welcome his grown son who has returned home after having shamefully squandered all his wealth. Elsewhere in the Bible, we read the truth that punctuates this story:

> Neither height nor depth, nor anything else in all creation, will be able to separate us from the love of God that is in Christ Jesus our Lord. (Rom. 8:39)

God's love for us looks like a barefoot and aging parent sprinting toward their child on a gravel road to throw their arms around them in relief. God loves us so much that God's love will always find us. Nothing can separate us from the home we have in God—not even the fog.

If you want to know what you're longing for, one telling place to look is your pain. Just as a coin has two sides, so does pain. Where there is pain, there is also longing.

The pain of a broken relationship might reveal our longing for love and nurture. The pain of being passed over for a promotion might reveal a longing to be valued and seen. The pain of being overworked might reveal a longing to rest and feel whole.

Because God wants to meet us in our pain, our longings help calibrate our coordinates for finding the way forward. The work of waking up is about leaning in to our longings and trusting that God meets us there. But how do we get in touch with our pain in a way that reveals our longings?

There is a collection of psalms—often called the pilgrim psalms—that capture this wayfinding. These are the songs of people in progress—those on a journey going from here to there, living in the in-between, and making their way toward a sacred place of being with God. Of these psalms, my favorite is Psalm 124. In part, it reads:

> Oh, blessed be GOD!
> He didn't go off and leave us.
> He didn't abandon us defenseless,
> helpless as a rabbit in a pack of snarling dogs.
> We've flown free from their fangs,
> free of their traps, free as a bird.
> Their grip is broken;
> we're as free as a bird in flight. (vv. 6–7 MSG)[4]

The climactic event in the Christian faith is the death and resurrection of Christ. The joy of Easter is vivid and bright because it comes in the wake of the unbearable pain of Good Friday.

The irony for us is that the painful places we work so hard to avoid are also the places we encounter God's love again and again. The places where we feel like we're as helpless as a rabbit in a pack of snarling dogs are the places we meet the cruciform Christ whose loving arms hold us and from whose presence we can set forth. God promises not to leave us in our pain; the hope of flight sustains us. The story of Jesus promises us that pain is not wasted in God's world, and what we long for matters as we make our way in the fog.

An Exercise for Waking Up

Maybe you're thinking, *But what if I don't know what I need to wake up to? How do I get in touch with what's beneath the surface if I'm not currently feeling disrupted?*

I know the feeling because I've been there myself.

In 2018, I gathered a group of eight women to beta test a program I designed to help cultivate entrepreneurial instincts in people who were oriented by their faith in Christ. It took me all of about five minutes into the first session to realize that exactly zero of them were there because they wanted to become more entrepreneurial. They were there because they wanted space—space to articulate the story of their own life, work on issues that left them feeling stuck, and ultimately move toward the person they sensed God calling them to be.

Influenced by the field of design thinking (which is essentially a philosophy for creating innovative products), I wondered what would happen if we helped people think creatively about their own vocation or their sense of God's calling in their lives. I created an exercise to help participants rapidly brainstorm pain points—the places of frustration, overwhelm, stuck-ness, or disappointment in their work or larger sense of vocation.[5] Today, this exercise has been run in countless team meetings, workshops, and cohort environments by many people beyond me.

I start by handing out a fresh stack of sticky notes and a good marker to everyone in the room. I instruct them to record their pain points on their sticky notes when the five-minute timer starts. (Just one per sticky note!) Because I'm usually working with people on issues related to work and leadership, I have them focus on work-related pain points. However, for the purposes of navigating your life when it's in flux, you can do this more broadly for yourself. Think about the pain points that feel acute, like the sting of a new cut, or ones that feel more chronic, like that pain in your hip that flares up every spring.

In those sessions, people start writing things like these:

my boss

feeling spread too thin

uncertain about what to do next

feeling overwhelmed

not enough money

impostor

the system wasn't built for me

parents' expectations

privilege

relational stress

anxiety

On and on, they write.

About halfway into the time, as the feverish scribbling inevitably slows down, I call out to them that it's important to keep writing for the entire five minutes, even if they find themselves sort of repeating thoughts or ideas. For many people, these remaining moments when they're rewriting the same thing in seventeen different ways can be a breakthrough. It's the pain points that surface again that seem to be the ones that need the most attention.

At the end of the five minutes, I ask participants to cluster their sticky notes into groups organized by themes that make sense to them. Because this is an exercise that's meant to help people individually, there really is no wrong way to do this. They just need to keep narrowing down until they have two or three pain points spelled out in front of them.

It's always quiet in the room at this point. It feels like a giant exhale, and most of those participating didn't even know they were holding their breath. They didn't realize they were holding so much unsurfaced pain inside.

The first couple of times I ran the exercise, I stopped it here. I asked people to pick a pain point they'd like to focus on for the rest of our time together, and then I moved on. But over time, I started to feel like the exercise was missing something and leaving people in a really tough place. I realized we needed not only a mechanism to help us name what wasn't working but also one to name where we wanted to go.

We had the *here*; we needed the *there*.

So, I added another step. After people narrow to two or three pain points, I now ask them to pull out some new blank sticky notes. Then I ask them to consider a question: What does each pain point reveal about what you're longing for?

At the time, the addition of this step had to do more with instinct about what was missing than a good theory on why we needed it. But now I've realized that, as Susan Cain says, "Longing is momentum in disguise."[6] This final step is a compass for finding the way forward. A way to deeply realign with our own sense of True North. A way to determine our own direction home.

When participants have their longings on sticky notes in a version they're ready to share, they stick their notes on the wall. As we take them in together, it's not uncommon for the sniffling sounds of tears to fill the room. Written on those notes is more than just our pain; it's our hope in the midst of it. This is what it looks like to be human. To, on the one hand, be so vividly marked by pain that it feels like we're among a pack of snarling dogs, while, on the other hand, we find ourselves longing with hope to be a bird in flight.

Take Lucy, for example. Her pain point was feeling spread too thin. She longed for a sense of deep rest. Or Maria, whose pain point was that she felt minimized by her boss. She longed for an invitation to take up more space in her work life. James found a pain point in that he had way too much responsibility. He longed to know more about what he should say yes and no to. Sasha was exhausted and longed for rest. Amy felt alone and longed for people who were truly on her side.

Over and over again, each pain was met with a longing. And each longing revealed an action step one could take to get there.

To wake up.

To find a new way forward.

To reach home again.

Your waking up starts by identifying the areas in your life where you feel pain. The places where you feel stuck, frustrated, or overwhelmed. As these places come to mind, it's helpful to recognize if the pain is chronic or acute. Has it been with you awhile? Or is it especially painful right now? It can also be helpful to assign a number to your pain points, with 1 representing a very mild pain point and 10 representing something that's very hard. By thinking of your pain points and going through this exercise, you can surface and acknowledge pain. Then, you can go to God and trust yourself as you ask, "What do these pain points reveal about what I am longing for?"

We all have longings that God has placed within us, but waking up to them is hard to do. Partly because the pain is so real, and partly because the future is often ambiguous. The tough news is that wading our way through ambiguity isn't easy or quick. The good news is that our willingness to wake up, see things differently, and get in touch with what we want deep down inside will help us find our way home in the fog.

A Prayer for When
It's Time to Wake Up

Lord,

It's easier to sleep.

There's too much pain to see.

Too many things to do.

Day in and day out.
A part of me is numb.

And yet . . .
a part of me is waking up
and wants to be more aware.
Something has to change.

I want more.
Help me to lift my head
and open my eyes.

Wake me up and
call me forth
into the fog,
the pain,
and the possibility.
Help me trust that waking up is good.

Amen.

Check Your Speed

Shauna's boss—let's call her Tiffany—was the actual worst.

At the senior level, Tiffany was vocal about her commitments to diversity, equity, inclusion, and belonging, and she championed the company's need to elevate women. But to those who reported up to her, she acted as a gatekeeper to opportunities. Time and time again, when Shauna was considered for project leadership or task force participation, Tiffany swooped in and gobbled up the opportunity for herself.

When Shauna decided she was ready to make a change, her friend recommended De Pree Center's Road Ahead program. The program is structured so that, in the second session, people get very deep about their vocational pain points and what those pain points reveal about what they're longing for. For Shauna, her pain point was that she felt undervalued, and it was impacting her confidence. When it came to assessing if she was a good fit for a new opportunity, Tiffany had really messed with her head. Embedded within this pain point was Shauna's deep desire to be a highly valuable member of a team and to have a boss who sought her best instead of blocking her growth.

As we went through the rest of our cohort, Shauna decided she wanted to have a very candid conversation with Tiffany. But as she got closer to enacting her plan, she felt like she just wasn't ready to go for it yet. Because a foundational value of the cohort is that people are there *to do the work they need to do*—nothing more or less—no one pushed Shauna to do something she was uncertain about. So, our cohort ended without her taking any concrete action toward her longing.

Truth be told, I felt like I had failed Shauna. I saw so much potential in her, but I couldn't help her take the risk she wanted to. Nine months later, I got a call from her that taught me something I'll never forget. She was calling to tell me that she had been accepted into graduate school for physical therapy and was about to quit her job. She planned to tell Tiffany about how horrible a boss she'd been, but she wanted to do it in a way that reflected her Christian values. She wanted to be candid but with grace and humility.

And she wanted to practice with me.

After Shauna had her script down, I asked her more about what had happened in the nine months after the cohort. She described a very slow, very cyclical process that included a lot of waking up as she pressed into the fog to hear God and come to know herself more deeply. As she did, she uncovered more and more that she wanted to dig into. She realized just how much of Tiffany's behavior she could control: none. She also came to reckon with deeper forces affecting her confidence—stuff from her childhood and a past romantic relationship. As it turned out, Tiffany was only the most recent person poking at deeper wounds that had been there much longer.

Shauna's work was slow, but it was also remarkable. Once she woke up to what she longed for, she never lost focus. She made her way, step-by-step, to an action plan that would not only help her deal with her boss but help her pursue what she really wanted. What looked like someone frozen in inaction was actually someone who intuitively knew to step back, slow down, and press deeper. Her pursuit didn't have quick results. Exploring what she had woken up to took her down an unexpected path that ultimately helped her realize Tiffany wasn't where she wanted to spend her best energy. Sure, she'd talk with her, but changing Tiffany's mind was not the focal point of her work.

The real work was becoming surer of who she was and who she wasn't.

NAVIGATIONAL SKILL #2:

Check Your Speed

I resist the near-constant external pressure to move fast so that I can do the slow, deep work that life in flux requires.

Setting the Pace

Making our way through the fog requires us to pace ourselves.

Boating on the ocean and navigating the waters around harbors, inlets, islands, and rivers requires understanding just how much conditions can vary and how to manage in different scenarios. For example, as we enter most harbor areas, or narrow channels, we will often see signs near the entrance that say "No Wake Zone." This is an indication that all boats must slow their speed so as not to produce a wake behind them—waves that will ripple out and inevitably cause other boats that are still to start rocking. The goal is to keep the waters in these areas flat and calm so heavier boating traffic can make safe passage and nearby kayakers don't get swamped.

The pace of navigating forward—toward God, our truest selves, and others—is slow, incremental, and focused work. It's *no wake zone* work that enables us to safely dock when we need to. If we're open to it, we'll spend our entire lives navigating home, and as we do so, we will be transformed along the way. The tough part is that, because modern life is lived at hyperspeed, we often do this deep, reflective work at the same time that we're actively traversing the raging waters of life. In light of this, I suggest the following rhythm (one learned from Roger's navigational skills) for checking our speed as we focus on deep, reflective work in the midst of everyday life.

1. Pause.

In nearly every corner of human life, things have sped up. In the midst of this, we honestly seem to be at odds with the very real constraints of our own humanity and the earth's rotation around the sun. Our desire to do more with the same amount of ourselves comes with very real costs.

We are caught in a vicious productivity trap. We sit in meetings while we answer our emails. We watch our kid's baseball games while we check the news. We answer texts from our friends or colleagues while we're in the bathroom. We are quite literally always doing something. And not only is that not good for our brains, it's the antithesis of the slow, small work that takes us home. Every time we demand more from ourselves, we weaken our ability to pause and make our way where we long to go.

At this point, there are many good studies on what our quest to do more is doing to our brains.[1] Take one very specific example: the efficiency of virtual meetings, accelerated by the global pandemic. A certain segment of our culture is now a work-from-anywhere culture.[2] And at the center of that culture is the virtual meeting.

Microsoft Human Factors Labs is a division of Microsoft that studies the impact of their products on humans. With the boom of virtual meetings, the team sought to understand the impact of back-to-back virtual meetings on the brain. Building on existing data, they monitored the brain activity of two different groups of people. One group had meetings back-to-back with no breaks. The other had the same number of meetings but with ten-minute breaks in between. They found that when participants move from meeting to meeting without breaks, their brains get tired, they have a hard time focusing, and they are stressed by the transition from one thing to the next.[3] (If you've ever sat in a multihour Zoom meeting, you probably feel like shouting "Duh!" right now.)

The research here is clear: not only is staring at screens hard for our brains but humans need breaks. Lots of them! Breaks are a good, healthy, and necessary part of what it means to be alive. We need time to transition from one thing to the next. If we don't slow down, we end up scattered, irritable, and anxious. And spoiler alert: without breaks, we also are far less productive.[4]

Of course, it's not just virtual meetings that are coming at us back-to-back. We're flooded with sources of information, ranging from news to meetings to social media, that demand our mental and emotional energy. In a meeting recently, a colleague leaned over my shoulder to tell me that my calendar looked unreasonable. She was right. I had my calendar overlaid with both my husband's personal calendar and our family calendar. It was completely overwhelming to look at, much less try to mentally manage. There, on my screen, it was all coming at me at once.

When things around us start moving faster, it's tempting to lean in hard to productivity hacks and time management tools in an effort to make space for more. (Hello, the calendars I just described!) The assumption is that because there's more coming at us and it's happening faster, we need to do more and go faster to keep up. But the data shows that when we implement these tricks and tools to try to master our time or get it back, we most often end up simply filling our new space with more stuff to do.[5] Oof.

What's at stake here is nothing small. In this work of making our way in the fog, the quick, efficient ways of moving simply will not do. Oliver Burkeman, writing for the *Wall Street Journal*, sums up the efficiency conundrum this way: "I'm aware of no other time management technique that's half as effective as just facing the way things truly are."[6] Facing things the way they are—with our very real and natural human limitations—is really the only thing that can and should be done.

We cannot frenetically make our way through life in flux. It simply won't work. Trust me, though: this is good news. Our humanity is good news. Our limits are good news. They force us to choose a new way forward, limitations and all. But, of course, that is easier said than done.

When we're in the midst of disorientation, counterintuitive shifts are often needed. We have to move slowly and differently. As we start making these shifts, we often don't feel productive, and the path certainly doesn't promise to be linear. When things are in flux, it's often unclear what we ought to focus on. The fire at work? The meltdowns at home? Our own health? Instead of focusing on what we can actually have agency over, we focus on everything, everywhere, all at once.[7]

We get trapped in reactive cycles (just reacting instead of paus-ing) when we get sideswiped or triggered by an event or a person. Think of it like getting punched and immediately punching back. Let's say I learn that one of my coworkers told someone else that he sees me as aggressive. My immediate knee-jerk reaction is probably defensiveness. *What does he know? He never listens to anyone!* I might shoot back with some comments about gendered expectations in the workplace or why he's the *real* problem.

Brain science calls this an amygdala hijack, where the part of the brain that processes information is bypassed and the part that senses danger and is wired to protect takes over.[8] It is often described as the "fight or flight" response, though many therapists and counselors add *freeze* to this list too. Picture a deer in the headlights—someone who ignores emotions completely or turns toward people-pleasing and numbing behaviors. Whether we tend toward fight, flight, or freeze, it's easy to react without thinking.

It's easy to skip over the much-needed pause.

Now, to be clear, there is a broad continuum of things that trigger us and push our buttons. Some of these are minor annoyances and others are the result of significant and harmful trauma—physical, emotional, and spiritual. I am not suggesting you can simply pause and breathe when something occurs that surfaces deep pain from past trauma you are still working through or may not even be aware of yet. As you start to notice your reactions, you are also creating fertile ground for deeper therapeutic needs to emerge. Lisa and I firmly believe in the power of therapy, spiritual direction, mentorship, and deep friendship. If you need to seek out that help as you process your way forward, please take time to do so.

Back on the boat on that foggy day, if Roger Slayton had jumped into action without pausing to consider the situation, who knows just how off course the boat would have drifted. Who knows how much time and precious gas he might have wasted. In order to get where he needed to go, setting the right pace was critical. And to do that, he had to start by pausing. As we seek to make our way through life in flux, honing the ability to pause is just as key for us.

As much as we want to rush the process of the way forward, we simply cannot. We must sit in the fog as we allow our old habits and beliefs to become unglued, examined, and eventually released. In order to endure flux, we must be willing to change.

COMMON POSTURE: I am focused on what I don't want and move in light of it.

UNCOMMON POSTURE: I am focused on what I do want and move in light of it.

If we can cultivate a habit of pausing and simply breathing for a moment or two when something unexpected happens, we'll begin to move out of reactivity and allow our brains to start processing again. As we shift from reacting in the face of danger to processing information, we tap into our own agency to move in the direction we want to. Instead of moving toward everything, everywhere, all at once, we move toward True North.

We move toward home.

2. Cut the engine.

It's one thing to pause. It's another to completely cut the engine—to quiet the noise of our lives enough so that we can listen for the signals of home. Our ability to cut the engine is tied to both our capacity to be at home in flux and our relationship with productivity or work.

In 2019, journalist Derek Thompson wrote a piece for the *Atlantic* that I've thought about nearly every week since.[9] It's titled "Workism Is Making Americans Miserable." In the piece, he argues that, as a culture, we've evolved into people who glean significance from and, in turn, worship what we do for paid work. He calls this *workism* and offers this as a definition for his term: "Workism is the belief that work is not only necessary to economic production, but also the centerpiece of one's identity and life's purpose."[10] In order to be able to regularly and decidedly cut the engine, we need to get clear about how we want to relate to work.

COMMON POSTURE: I am what I do. My work defines me.

UNCOMMON POSTURE: I am a whole person. My work is a part of who I am but does not define me.

For most of human history, work has served a primarily utilitarian purpose—a means through which we have access to food, shelter, and other basics for the rest of life. That's not to say that people haven't enjoyed work throughout the ages; it's just that work as a means of self-expression wasn't the *deeper* aim. But now, as author Jonathan Malesic says, "Work sits at the heart of Americans' vision of human flourishing. It's much more than how we earn a living. It's how we earn dignity: the right to count in society and enjoy its benefits."[11]

Not only does this read like a gut punch of privilege and rugged individualism gone wild but it stands in contrast to a biblical vision of what human flourishing looks like.

We need to decide if we are okay with this.

That's not to say that work isn't good; it's just not the whole picture or the basis on which we earn the right to count. And if, deep down, we believe that, then there's room for us to develop a different relationship with rest.

There's room for us to start cutting our engine.

It's important to name here that because work shows up in the garden in Genesis with God and the first people *before* sin, we can be sure work is not a result of sin. Yes, when human sin entered the picture it brought with it exploitation, coercion, and greed. Yes, work has been a vehicle in which these evil forces have played out in dramatic fashion. But in its first and purest form, work is a good and creative gift from God.

However, work doesn't always feel like that good gift from God, does it? At any point in recent years (pandemic years included), one could do a quick online search to see how many people disliked or were disengaged in their jobs. The numbers have hovered between 40 and 80 percent. In 2021, this perennial statistic took on new form with "The Great Resignation," which was a way to describe a state of American life in which 40 to 60 percent of people actively considered quitting their jobs.[12] Then came "quiet quitting," where up to 50 percent of the American workforce did not technically quit their jobs but instead stepped back from going above and beyond in them.[13]

On top of this, here in the United States, we are a people who celebrate productivity. We glamorize getting stuff done, even if we hate it. Take these recent statistics, for example: 85 percent of men and 66 percent of women work more than forty hours per week.[14] More than half of US workers report not using all their vacation days.[15] And 49 percent of Americans under age thirty-five report having a side hustle.[16] Some of this is surely the result of underemployment and low wages. Consider the person who has a full-time job and a part-time gig just to make things work financially. Their side hustle isn't a choice not to rest; it's a necessity to pay the bills. But there's another layer here, and that's the fact that our society rewards productivity. We tip our proverbial caps when people seem to be winning at this game. We hashtag #goals and #hustle. The logic goes that if work is a context in which we achieve meaning (which we're wired to crave), then doing *more work* must be *more meaningful*, right?

Deep down, we can feel that America's relationship to work isn't working. We're overextended and exhausted, and some of us are deeply unhappy because of our work. That reality doesn't feel aligned with the notion that work is a good and creative gift from God. It's in the midst of all this that, as believing people in these particular and peculiar times, we turn our attention to God and toward one another, asking and hoping for another way.

Our quest for the way forward takes us back to the book of Exodus, which is about how God delivers the Israelites out of slavery and into the promised land. Along the way, we see a stark contrast between the ways of Pharaoh's kingdom and the ways of the kingdom of God.

Let's start with Pharaoh. In Exodus 1:8–14, driven by fear of the growing population of Israelites in Egypt, Pharaoh treated them harshly. In essence, he believed either they conquered the Israelites or the Israelites would conquer them. One people would have control, and one people wouldn't. One would win, and one would lose. In Exodus 5, Pharaoh instructs his taskmasters to no longer give the enslaved Israelites straw to make bricks but rather to require them to both gather the straw and build the bricks themselves. He made this change all while keeping the brick quotas the same. The implicit message here is that the enslaved people would need to work longer, faster, and harder. They'd need to do more—work more—in an already unjust situation.

As Pharaoh's reign goes on, the Exodus story gets pretty dramatic. Of course, God eventually delivers the Israelites, and Moses leads them out of Egypt. So, in Exodus 20, when God gives them the Ten Commandments, God is helping the Israelites imagine just how different God's kingdom is from Pharaoh's. This is part of those commandments:

> Remember the Sabbath day by keeping it holy. Six days you shall labor and do all your work, but the seventh day is a sabbath to the LORD your God. On it you shall not do any work, neither you, nor your son or daughter, nor your male or female servant, nor your animals, nor any foreigner residing in your towns. For in six days the LORD made the heavens and the earth, the sea, and all that is in them, but he rested on the seventh day. Therefore, the LORD blessed the Sabbath day and made it holy. (Exod. 20:8–11)

In these four verses, we see just how stark the contrast is between God's rule and Pharaoh's. Under Pharaoh's reign, work was exploitative and harsh. It was driven by fear, anxiety, and greed. Pharaoh's kingdom was an either/or kingdom. Either he controlled the Israelites, or they would rise up against him. Either he exploited and coerced them for profit, or he would be seen as weak. Either they worshiped him and were subject to his rule, or they were a threat to his power.

Now, in contrast, God restores rhythm and godly order to work. I say *restores* because God first modeled this rhythm of work and rest in the beginning. In Genesis, we have a depiction of God as Maker. God worked to make the heavens and earth, to separate the night from the day, to fashion dry land and separate it from the seas, and of course, to call into existence plants, birds, and every living creature, including humans. As part of this rhythm, Genesis 2:2–3 reveals that God, having finished this monumental work of making, settled into a period of rest.

In other words, God cut the engine to take a moment to be still.

Now, it wasn't that God was exhausted from the work. No, God saw rest as a good and right thing to do after all the making. In this, we see that in God's kingdom there is a cadence that feels so wildly different from Pharaoh's. If Pharaoh's kingdom is either/or, God's kingdom is both/and. There is both an expectation of work and a promise of rest. Both an invitation to make and one to pause. Both an opportunity to participate in what God is doing and one to remember that we are not God.

Importantly, in Exodus we see that the Sabbath commandment has a neighborly dimension too. Sabbath is not an invitation for individuals. It is not either for you or for someone else. No, it is both for you and for your neighbors. Work is communal, and therefore so is rest. In this command to consider others, God disrupts any bit of the Israelite imagination that has been shaped by Pharaoh-like greed.

Work is good and therefore should not be exploited.

Rest is necessary and therefore must be protected for all.

COMMON POSTURE: Sabbath exists so I have time to recover from a long and hard work week.

UNCOMMON POSTURE: Sabbath is a gift—a time to rest and delight in God.

The question for us today is this: Are we living and working by the rhythm of Pharaoh's either/or kingdom or the rhythm of God's both/and kingdom? Of course, this is complicated because we are human people living in the midst of multiple kingdoms. We are citizens of the kingdom of God that invites us to good and fruitful rhythms of both work and rest. Yet we live here on earth surrounded by so much, including many Pharaoh-like forces fueled by anxiety and greed.

a "profit at all cost" mentality

an "always on" culture

racism

sexism

workism

I'm sure you could name other Pharaoh-like forces that can and do compel us to work at all costs, never settle for less than more, exploit others along the way, and worship what we do. Forces that demand we always keep the engine going.

For this reason, it's been helpful for me to think about Sabbath both as an act of resistance and as a good gift to receive.[17] Sabbath defies the forces of Pharaoh at play in our human world. It empowers us to resist anything that tells us that production is more important than people or that meaning is found in accumulation. Sabbath is also a gift in that we can't *achieve* truly transformative rest but rather only *receive* it from God. Receiving God's gift of rest (and all that happens in it) is our declaration that work is not the primary place where we seek fulfillment.

Here's the kicker. Most believing Christians already know about God's invitation to work and rest. The idea of Sabbath is not new. Yet it feels so hard to practice or access that we don't always do it. We stop short of understanding its systemic and neighborly dimensions.

What if, together, we resisted the idea that work is the *sole* container for meaning? What if that was our protest to Pharaoh-like forces at play? What if both rest and work were our places of meaning-making? What if we took seriously that God is at work restoring the world, and that our practice of the rhythm of work and rest is integral to our capacity to align with God? What if that is part of what it means to live, and work, and lead distinctively as Christians in these particular and peculiar times?

What if Sabbath is what it looks like to cut the engine?

One of the ways we can do this is to build in structured rhythms of rest in our lives. This will look different depending on the season we're in, and that's okay. When I was in my twenties, rest might have been a four-hour hike with friends. As a new mom, rest might have meant hiding my phone, taking deep breaths, and staring at the ceiling while my baby napped.

When we learn to slow down and pause regularly, it becomes more possible to go to that space when life feels like it's in flux.

Lisa and I have a mutual friend named Joan. She is a high-powered professional married to another high-powered professional, Sam. Beyond their two big jobs, they have three teenage kids, four aging parents, two large extended families, two dogs, and a host of commitments related to church and community life.

In other words, life is *very* full.

The incredibly competent people they are, they make choices based on how to optimize their scarcest resource: time. Going on the rare date night? Well, let's get the car washed on the way and stop at the grocery store for a few things on the back end. We'll take car A so that the kids can take car B out with their friends. If we get home before 10:00 p.m., we'll be able to catch our teenagers before they go to their rooms for the night. Then, we can do a little work before we go to bed.

For years, they made their choices based on how to optimize their time.

Until one day they stopped.

Feeling the weight of such a high-performance lifestyle, they were burned out and unhealthy physically, as well as both on the verge of a mental breakdown. Their therapist recommended that they take three months and intentionally *not* optimize their time.

The car might be dirty.

The kids would eat whatever was in the house for breakfast.

No work would be done before bed.

Together, they were going to slow down—big time.

The first month was ROUGH. The second was settling. By the third, they felt like they were rediscovering each other, sleeping better, and gaining needed perspective on the cost fast-paced living had taken on their souls. They paused in a particular way for a few months, and it gave them the insight they needed to reimagine how the next decade of their lives might look and to develop a new rhythm going forward.

Cutting the engine in one area helps us grow insight for how we might do it in another. Regularly getting quiet enough to listen helps us know how to do so when we feel blindsided by disruption or change.

3. Listen for signals.

The navigational sounds of the ocean are fascinating.

Foghorns warn ships of nearing obstacles that are no longer visible in the mist or the fog. These sounds are made electronically by now-automated lighthouses. Many ships can produce them as well. Different intervals between sounds and ranging quantities of sound blasts signal different things, helping indicate where the not-visible obstacle is located. For example, the closer you are to the obstacle, the louder the sound and shorter the interval. Any captain who hears this knows they are in danger.

Bell buoys are bells attached to very large buoys anchored at key locations to mark channels, outcroppings of sunken ledges, and harbor or river entrances. The rougher the seas, the louder and more insistent the bells. An experienced boater knows how to make sense of all these sounds when visibility is low, making constant small course corrections along the way. When Roger was lost in the fog, he was experienced enough to know not only to listen for these familiar sounds but to estimate his distance from them and correct his course each time he paused and cut the engine.

We must learn to do the same.

As we meet inevitable disorientation, over time we can develop the same awareness to listen to the signals of our lives to guide us forward through an ever-changing world. Doing so allows us to be present, understand complexity, and discover how God might be guiding us in the confusion. The spiritual practices that help us slow and learn to listen to the sounds beneath the noise are of vital importance here. One practice I've observed to be particularly helpful is *contemplation*.

Richard Rohr and his team define the practice this way: "Contemplation is the practice of being fully present—in heart, mind, and body—to what is in a way that allows you to creatively respond and work toward what could be."[18] Dr. Barbara Peacock, who writes about soul care in African American practice, adds that contemplation is about exalting and drawing power and strength from God, becoming a vessel through which God can work.[19]

Peacock holds up Dr. Rosa Parks as a prime example of contemplation in action. You likely know Parks's courageous story of sitting silently, refusing to give up her seat for a white person on a bus in Montgomery, Alabama, in 1955. Her simple but profound act of resistance was a catalyst for the growing Civil Rights Movement. Peacock says it was a deep well of long-practiced contemplation that gave Parks "unusual spiritual determination"[20] to occupy a seat, an action that she knew full well would spark a strong and perhaps even violent response. It was her nurtured sense of God's peace that carried her into that moment and through it, arguably making her one of the most vital spiritual leaders for the entire movement.

Most of us will not lead a movement as Dr. Parks did, but we will find ourselves in countless difficult situations that require us to be deeply calibrated to God's guidance and love. When we regularly practice connecting to God in a way that deepens our awareness, we're practicing *listening to the signals.* To know in a contemplative way is much less about what the brain decides and much more about, as Rohr says, "holistic, heart centered knowing, where mind, heart, soul, and senses are open and receptive to the moment just as it is."[21]

Change does not submit to our will. Even when we make choices, we are subject to the force of transition. As we inevitably are tossed around in the sea of life, our sense of being grounded (or lack thereof) impacts how we hear and therefore how we move forward.

4. Move incrementally forward.

When we know the direction we want to go, the temptation is to move quickly toward that horizon. But if we do that, we aren't pacing ourselves. What if we need to recalibrate along the way? What if new factors enter the picture? The only way to truly make our way to where we want to go is step-by-step. This happens when we focus on small, doable steps. When we embrace that the small things are really the big things.

71

This happens when we move incrementally forward.

We never really know how long the fog will last. Some seasons are short, others are long. Some are intense, others less so. It's difficult work experiencing the pain that comes with change without numbing ourselves to it.

In my experience, this happens most productively when we try to do only a little bit at a time. This is why it's been helpful for me to think about *next doable risks*.[22] A next doable risk is something you can do with the resources you already have, like your time, your energy, a relationship, money, or an opportunity. It's a risk in that whatever you choose to do requires you to step into an unknown future, but doing so will help you learn more about how to move incrementally forward.

Taking It Slow

Let's go back to Shauna. When she was part of our cohort, I thought her next doable risk was to have a hard conversation with Tiffany. Obviously, I was wrong. That was too big and potentially too costly. But just because it wasn't time for that specific conversation didn't mean she wasn't moving forward incrementally. She decided she wanted something to change (risk #1) and that she was going to take steps toward a new horizon. She joined a cohort (risk #2), talked things through with others (risk #3), and made a plan (risk #4). Then she paused, cut the engine to step back even further, and thought about her long-term goal (risk #5). She had countless conversations with people who loved her (risk #6) as she did the work of attuning to God in the fog and really getting to know herself (risk #7).

Then she was ready to make a bigger move.

She applied to three grad schools (risk #8) and got into two. After this, she was ready to exit her job with honesty and grace. So, she talked with Tiffany (risk #9), who was pretty defensive.

The difference? At this point, Tiffany's defensiveness didn't affect Shauna in the same way anymore. Through all her processing and incremental steps forward, she had grown in this season of flux. She was clear on what she wanted, what she needed to do, and what she didn't need to do.

Pause.

Cut the engine.

Listen for signals.

Move incrementally forward.

We have the power to choose how we respond. We *can* build new and healthier rhythms of work and rest that enable space for deep listening and intentional, incremental response. Learning to slow down in our lives helps us check our speed in any given situation. Pausing in this way will serve us well for a lifetime. We may have seasons where we speed up again for various reasons, but if we're wise, we'll quickly recognize any signals that tell us we're going too fast for too long. And if we do the work of checking our speed now, we'll have good tools and resources in place to shift gears. To pause or even push hard on the brakes. To pace ourselves as we move forward through and out of the fog.

A Prayer for Slowing Down

God, it feels impossible to go slow.
I run through the hours in a day
like a hamster on a wheel.
A never-ending list of tasks to finish,
people to respond to,
and projects to complete.

And yet, apart from you, they hold no meaning.
I declare that I am made in your image
as a human being, not a human doing.

You place your hand on my shoulder
and make me to lie down,
to rest by the water.

Why do I resist?
Why do I keep trying to get myself back up?

And yet, when I rest with you,
my body, my soul, my heart quiet and still,
renewed and refreshed.

Lead me toward your loving rest
no matter how many times I get it wrong.
Have mercy on my restless soul.

Show me a different way.

Amen.

Choose to Let Go

Several years ago, my husband, Dan, and I were driving to a friend's house to watch March Madness.[1] We were just a few blocks from our house when a large truck turned left and slammed into the side of our car. The force was so strong that our car flipped upside down. All our windows were shattered, the roof was smashed in, and we were left hanging upside down, strapped in by our seat belts. We remained there until a man whose name I'll never know lay belly down on a pile of glass, reached into our car, and pulled me out of the driver's side window.

To this day, it remains one of the scariest moments of my life.

Right before we were hit, time seemed to stand still. I can still remember feeling like I was waiting to get hit. I can still remember bracing myself for the crash. I don't understand how so much happened in that millisecond, but as I've talked with other crash victims, I've learned that it's a common experience. Time does, for whatever reason, seem to halt.

In that moment before impact, Dan said to me, "We're about to get hit. Lean in and let go!"

His advice was that of a skier trained to fall. Dan grew up skiing in the Salt Lake area and had explained to me that one of the chief goals when learning to ski is to learn how to fall and to excel at the same time. He says it's as if he learned to fall on the mountain before he learned to ski it. Because of that, he knew that falling requires letting go and relaxing your body. If you tense up or try to catch yourself along the way, your tighter muscles lead to more pain. But if you lean in and let go, you can endure most of what can happen when you fall.

Ironically, as skiers learn to let go in a fall, they develop the capacity to become more attuned to the momentum of their bodies. Thus, they can potentially position themselves better both physically and mentally. By letting go and tuning in to their bodies, they have a better chance of pulling their skis underneath them or recovering.

I, on the other hand, am a white-knuckler by default.

So, in the millisecond before our SUV got hit, I did not take Dan's advice. I did not let go. I did not work with the momentum of my body like an expert skier. No, I tensed up and braced myself. Many years later, I have ongoing pain from that crash, while Dan has none. I'm convinced it's because he was able to let go while I could not.

NAVIGATIONAL SKILL #3:
Let Go
*I release that which keeps me
from moving forward.*

If you've ever seen a trapeze artist flying through the air, then you've witnessed the breathtaking moment of suspense when they release one swing before grabbing onto another.

In that moment, they are suspended.

While they are seemingly weightless high above the ground, as an audience, we're suspended with them. We're subject to any number of our own emotions, perhaps even simultaneously. We might cover our eyes, unable to bear the tension and terrified they will fall. We might lean forward on the edge of our seats, holding our breath with anticipation and hope. We might cry out or laugh, overcome with the suspense of it all.[2]

For many of us, letting go feels absolutely terrifying.

> **COMMON POSTURE:** I keep white-knuckling, even after I sense that my way is not working.
>
> **UNCOMMON POSTURE:** I let go, trusting God and embracing whatever comes next.

Letting go isn't something we can first decide to do in a moment of crisis. The trapeze artist cannot do a trick for the very first time at a sold-out show. I couldn't learn to let go in the face of an oncoming collision. We can't learn to fall as we're falling. If we have not trained and practiced those instincts over time, they won't be there in the heat of the moment. They won't help us when life is in flux.

Here's the thing: without the ability to let go, we'll inevitably revert back to our old ways—even if we've just woken up to the fact that they won't get us where we want to go.[3] In his book *Necessary Endings*, psychologist and author Henry Cloud writes, "For us to ever get to a new level, a new tomorrow, or the next step, something has to end. Life has seasons, stages, and phases. For there to be anything new, old things always have to end, and we have to let go of them."[4]

In order to make our way through flux, we must be willing to change. And in order to change, we must learn to let go. We see this developmentally with babies who become toddlers who grow into children who eventually become adults. We see it in the rhythms of the seasons as the autumn gives way to a winter that spring promises to follow. And we see it when we learn to let go of that which traps us in reactivity loops or leaves us feeling stuck for the long term.

Learning to Let Go

During a challenging financial season at the organization where Lisa had worked for many years, the board of directors decided to make a leadership change and asked her to step in as the interim president. A self-described rescuer driven by a sense of outsized responsibility, she agreed. Lisa spent the first sixty days on a listening tour—asking people about the work of the organization and what they thought needed to happen next. As she did, she immediately found herself with much more than a financial issue on her hands. By listening to people's stories, she discovered there were really tough and destructive relational dynamics at play among key stakeholders in the organization. Because of this, the organization's reputation had taken a hit among both stakeholders and folks in the larger community.

A few months into this interim role, Lisa was completely overwhelmed. Her proverbial boat was taking on too much water, and she had no good way to bail it out. She was deep in the fog—with no clear picture of what to do next.

Not really knowing what to do, she called her close friend, who also happened to be involved with the organization. Let's call him Sam. She relayed the results of her listening tour, breaking the news that the current way she, the staff, and the board were functioning wasn't working. Not only was it unsustainable financially but people were siloed, and there weren't effective communication channels.

Sam's response surprised her. In short, he told Lisa he didn't see a problem at all. She was simply blowing things out of proportion.

Lisa was heartbroken, not to mention exhausted, frustrated, and now confused. While she didn't quite have the words for it at the time, she could sense that the skills that had gotten her to where she was weren't going to get her out of the fog. Her internal narrative of self-reliance, which worked so well elsewhere, was simply not working now. In order to navigate forward, she needed to do something different.

But she didn't, at least not at first. Instead, Lisa thought she could convince people to change, and that's what she kept trying to do. It was only after several difficult conversations with stakeholders, in which the needle didn't budge, that one of the other members, Dave, told Lisa a hard truth.

He said, "You're allowing this system to define you."

What followed those words was a monthslong journey of letting go.

At first, Lisa wasn't quite sure what Dave's comment meant, but she could feel it was true. She was starting to sense that her own rescuing tendencies caused her to over-function in an effort to please everyone, even as she felt like she was drowning. She was trying to white-knuckle the way forward at all costs.

As it turned out, there was a lot she needed to let go of:

unhealthy relationships

a limited internal narrative about who she was

her own coping behaviors

the need to be in control

Her ability to navigate a very disruptive season rested on her willingness to grow. As the person in charge, she felt it was counterintuitive to let go. But because nothing else was working, what other choice did she have?

So, she started unclenching her fists.

As she slowly released her grip on relationships and the need to be in control, she felt a lot like that trapeze artist, suspended in the in-between and, at the same time, still very much subject to the rhythms of normal life.

She became awake to more. She started cutting the engine and taking incremental steps forward. Slowly, she began to make her way in the fog.

Though the details are her own, Lisa's story is not uncommon. In our work, she and I see five recurring themes when it comes to what many of us need to let go of.

1. The stories and habits that got us here.

What got us here isn't necessarily bad; it just might not serve us as life is in flux. Sure, some of our habits are unhealthy and need to be released, like saying yes to projects and requests that overextend us. But other times, it's more nuanced. It might be that the compete-with-myself mindset that got us through graduate school now stands in the way of expressing gratitude to our teammates. It may have served us before, but now we have to let it go.

2. The coping behaviors and skills we have developed for self-protection.

Over time, we all develop habits we believe will keep us safe and secure when life is in flux. These may include becoming distant or aloof when things get challenging or, alternatively, heating up and becoming angry or judgmental. Of course, we have all the numbing behaviors to deal with too. Bingeing TV, overeating, drinking, shopping—we pick our poison. We put up barriers between us and other people to keep from getting hurt, but that also keeps us distant from the relationships we need most. We have to let go of the things we think are protecting us in order to move forward. It's human to need to cope with uncertainty and change, but the very behaviors we set up to protect ourselves are an obstacle on the path forward.

3. The beliefs that limit us.

We all have thoughts that have settled in as deeply held beliefs. Sometimes that's for the better, but often these hold us back. *I am only worth what I produce* or *I have to find the perfect job/spouse/ friend group/house to be happy* aren't the kinds of thoughts that ground us during change. They aren't doing anything to help us move forward when things feel uncertain. Once we begin to uncover and examine these beliefs in the light of day, they can be renarrated based on the truths of Scripture, which offers a new kind of freedom. For example, *I have worth and dignity because I belong to God, not because of what I do* or *I find my contentment in Christ, not in my circumstances.*

4. The unhealthy relationships we have with individuals or systems.

When Dave told Lisa, "You're allowing this system to define you," it was a light bulb moment for her. Because she was a lifelong rescuer and people pleaser, her default mode was to identify the person or persons in an organization whose expectations mattered most. Then she would set about doing whatever was needed to meet those expectations. She had several relationships built on this dynamic that were causing her to operate way outside of who she was and how she could contribute best. As she learned to set boundaries and identify which expectations were realistic and which were not, she had to slowly let go of the relationships in which these boundaries and new ways of engaging were not respected or honored.

5. The need to control.

Control is about keeping ourselves safe. More often than we'd like to admit, it's based in fear. We fear being controlled, being taken advantage of, being trapped in pain, or being harmed in some way. While our individual fears may be different, they breed the same need for control.[5] When we are grasping for control, we cannot engage in healthy relationships, trust, or collaboration. We often work against the very things we say we want because the intensity of our fear keeps us from being present to ourselves and others. Control is not *always* bad or unhealthy, but when it creates highly restrictive boundaries that keep us out of relationships and the love God has for us in the midst of flux, then control has to be released and healed.[6]

> **COMMON POSTURE:** I stay attached to habits, patterns, and rhythms that no longer serve me but feel familiar.
>
> **UNCOMMON POSTURE:** I release habits, patterns, and rhythms that no longer serve me and slowly replace them with new ways of being, doing, and showing up.

For months on end, Lisa cried in church every Sunday. As she did, she sensed God inviting her into a new way of being. This incredibly disruptive crisis—in which everything she knew to be true felt in flux—was also an opportunity for her to relearn to be a human *being*, not just a human *doing*.

As Lisa slowly and reluctantly let go of the story that she could save the day, let go of the impulse to take charge too quickly, and let go of her desire to control people and circumstances, she also put herself at the start of a journey of really learning to trust God and a close circle of friends. She engaged her own team of support in the form of an executive coach, a therapist, and a spiritual director who, over time, helped her let go of all that she was white-knuckling.

Stepping Back and Letting Go

Oftentimes, letting go happens after we pause and step back. Leadership experts call this "getting on the balcony."[7] We spend so much of our time and energy on the proverbial dance floor of life, but while on the floor it can be hard to gain perspective. We can't see how the actions we take impact others or if we're off-rhythm from the music. By stepping back and getting on the balcony, our perspective widens. We can not only see what's going on across the entire dance floor but gain insight into how our actions impact others.

Rather than busying ourselves with activity or over-functioning, we learn to stop, cut the engine, listen, and wait until we have a clear sense of how to proceed forward. As we learn to do this, we get clearer and clearer, not only about who we are but also about the work that is really ours to do (and the work that's not!). As we take small step after small step back, we're often simultaneously, ever so slowly, letting go.

One of the most difficult parts of stepping back is that we see what's causing our worry and anxiety more clearly. With that comes a difficult part of letting go: shifting our energy away from that which we are anxious about but have very little control over.

You might feel upset about a client who sends you a demanding email after hours. Or you may be overwhelmed by your sister-in-law who has too many toxic traits to list. Or you could be anxious because you send your kids to school in a country where we have an epidemic of gun violence. In each of these instances, you don't really have control over what other people do. You can only control how you show up in the world and respond to the frustrating, overwhelming, or frightening parts of life. The rest? Well, you have the agency to let it go.

One of the most helpful ways to start to let go of the things we worry about but don't actually have control over is by visualizing them. Consider the image below, which was first popularized by leadership author Stephen Covey in the late 1980s. His original illustration has been adapted and improved on millions of times and used widely over the years as a helpful tool to get clear on where we should focus our attention.[8]

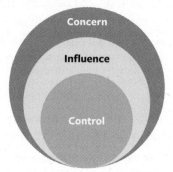

In these concentric circles, the outer circle is the circle of concern, where we place all those things that we care about but have no ability to directly affect. The middle ring is the circle of influence, where we place things we may be able to affect and that deserve some energy and attention. Finally, the inner circle is the place where we actually can control what happens.

Commonly, we spend an inordinate amount of energy on things in the outermost circle—things we're concerned about but cannot control or even influence. This is often heightened when our personal or professional lives feel in flux.

The more we shift our energy and attention to the inner circle, the more we'll be able to reduce our worry, anxiety, and stress. And the more we'll be able to let go of what is hindering us when things are changing and the future is uncertain.

Of course, we cannot do this without first stepping back to become aware of where we're focused and what it's costing us. Once we do, however, we can shift our thinking. Understanding this paradigm can help us change the way we perceive and show up to all types of situations.

For example, I might move away from thoughts like this: *My sister-in-law is so toxic! She's the worst.* (Full disclosure: my sister-in-law is an amazing human, but you get the point.) Then I can move toward thoughts like this: *I know I can only be around my sister-in-law in limited doses. So, during a family gathering, I need to take breaks for myself and communicate about those breaks in clear and loving ways to my partner.*

One way to identify the different things in each circle is to list all the things that are on your mind today. Include everything causing you to worry or feel stressed. Your list may include things in your political, economic, work, family, or community realms. Make the list (at least the first time!) as exhaustive as possible.

my grocery list
bullying at my kid's school
racism in my city
how my presentation went yesterday
my narcissistic colleague

Once you have created your list, ask yourself the following questions for each item to determine if it should receive a red, yellow, or green check:

- Is this in the past or the future? If so, give it a red check.
- Is this related to the actions or opinions of others? Red check.
- Is this related to things happening or circumstances around me? Red check.
- Is this related to how others take care of themselves? Red check.
- Is this related to things in the present? If so, give it a yellow check.

- Is it related to the people I lead or interact with regularly? Yellow check.

- Is it related to the systems I work within? Yellow check.

- Is it related to the circumstances I directly affect? Yellow check.

- Is it related to my thoughts and actions? If so, give it a green check.

- Is it related to how I react or respond? Green check.

- Is it related to where I am focusing my energy and attention? Green check.

- Is it related to the boundaries I have in place with others? Green check.[9]

If you have mostly red and yellow checks, then you're likely focusing enormous amounts of energy on things that may concern you (red) or that perhaps you can influence (yellow) but over which you have very little actual control. Only the things on your list that got green checks are things you can directly control. Take note that these green checks are focused on how you manage yourself. Not others, not politicians, not even the latest natural disaster. These things genuinely deserve our concern, and there may be things we can do in small ways to affect them. But generally, day in and day out, we can really only manage ourselves. It's when we come to terms with this reality that we can move forward from a place of peace, not fear and anxiety. It's not that we never think about gun violence, or how racism impacts our kids, or if an economic recession is looming. It's that we reframe how we engage these things. We should continue to be concerned, and we can influence the way forward, but rarely can we singlehandedly control outcomes.

Getting this enables us to let go.

The Grief of Letting Go

At its core, letting go is grief work. Of course, grief comes in all shapes and sizes. On the one hand, we know exactly what grief feels like, and on the other, it's hard to put our finger on it. In writing this book, Lisa and I asked people online to share their metaphors for grief. Here's a sampling of their responses:

> Grief sometimes comes with force, like a raging storm at sea—terrifyingly pervasive without any hope of escape.
>
> Grief is a lightning bolt, jolting us out of reality as time stands still.
>
> It can be a bit like glitter, in that once you think you've cleared it all away, you still find little pieces of grief when you least expect it.
>
> Grief is like a small child demanding our full attention.
>
> Grief is an unresolved music note just hanging in the air.

The work of emotional intelligence (often referred to as EQ) has become foundational to many leadership and organizational theories since Daniel Goleman published his landmark work, *Emotional Intelligence: Why It Can Matter More Than IQ*, in the midnineties. He broadly describes emotional intelligence as the ability to identify, understand, and manage one's own emotions as well as recognize and influence the emotions of others.[10] He argues that, while IQ is important, EQ is a key predictor of success in life, and identifies five components of emotional intelligence: self-awareness, self-regulation, motivation, empathy, and social skills. By developing these five skills, Goleman says, individuals can improve their personal and professional relationships and perform higher in their careers.

But there's a catch.

If we're not careful, we'll end up being smart about our feelings at the cost of actually *feeling* our feelings. Being smart about emotions isn't the same as being able to deal with them. If we're thinking about our feelings and thinking that thinking counts as feeling, we will miss the necessary work that happens in the messy, ambiguous, raging sea, lightning bolt kind of feelings.

We cannot tame grief.

Goodness, do we still try.

Miriam Greenspan argues that as a society we've never actually been good at taming any of the emotions we deem negative. Escaping? Yes. Coping? Yes. But taming? No. She describes grief, fear, and despair—which she clusters as dark emotions—as emotions commonly regarded as negative. Therefore, they're repressed and avoided at all costs, which only means they show up as depression, anxiety, addiction, irrational violence, and numbing.[11] In short, more white-knuckling. She writes, "While generally devalued in our culture, the dark emotions have a wisdom that is essential to the work of healing and transformation on both individual and collective levels."[12]

Most of us are probably familiar with Elisabeth Kübler-Ross's five stages of grief: denial, anger, bargaining, depression, and acceptance.[13] What we might not know is that these stages of grief were originally meant to apply to the dying, not the living. Kübler-Ross's work explored the experience of dying by studying terminally ill patients.[14] Her work is rightfully hailed as ushering in a shift in the way we talk about dying. As it is no longer taboo, medical and layfolk alike now have language that resonates with dying patients.

Of course, the five stages of grief have become ubiquitous far beyond the context of dying patients. That's not all bad, as the language and framing are good tools for us. What's more worrisome is the thought that's been born out of these stages: the belief that grief is something that can be structured or has milestones to be hit. This just doesn't work. Grief is like glitter. We find it in the crevices of our lives long after we assumed it was all cleaned up.

"Get closure," we're told, but so much of life is not cut and dried. Sometimes what we need to let go of leaves us feeling unresolved— like a music note just hanging in the air. This is almost always true when we're letting go of that which keeps us stuck.

Pauline Boss is a renowned family therapist and former professor at the University of Minnesota who is known for her groundbreaking work on *ambiguous loss*, or losses that are unclear or unresolved. Consider a child who has cut off contact from their parents, a parent who has Alzheimer's, a divorce after which you still coparent, or an alcoholic sibling who becomes a different person when they drink.[15] This type of pain isn't easily resolved, and neither is the grief that comes with it.

Our grief itself can be in flux.

American society prefers to keep grief in a box, so it makes sense that appropriating Kübler-Ross's framework for the dying onto anything we're going through feels neat and sensible. If we can frame it, we can control it. But what if Boss's framework is actually what we need? Because life in flux promises more volatile, complex, uncertain, and ambiguous ruptures, we need an understanding of grief that is less restricted and more spacious.

We need frameworks that help us navigate the fog.

Grief can't read a calendar. It doesn't know when it's bedtime. That means it doesn't wait until things are convenient or quiet. We might be working on letting go of the stories we've told ourselves for so long amid the backdrop of a world war breaking out. Or we might be saying goodbye to the coping behaviors we've relied on while collectively reckoning with systemic injustice in our time. Grief doesn't care what's happening in or around us; it simply shows up and demands our attention. And when *the* world and *our* worlds are in flux, it gets all the more complex.

In an interview she sat for with the *New York Times* during the height of the pandemic, Boss offered six nonsequential guidelines meant to help people bear their grief:

make meaning out of loss
relinquish one's desire to control an uncontrollable situation
re-create identity after loss
become accustomed to ambivalent feelings
redefine one's relationship with whatever or whomever they've lost
find new hope[16]

Because letting go can feel so counterintuitive and unclear—like we're pushing deeper into the fog—it's important to have guidelines that help us hear the sounds of home. For the record, Boss's are good ones. When we need to let go of the stories we've told ourselves for so long, it's helpful to orient ourselves toward becoming accustomed to ambivalent feelings. Or when we're trying to let go of coping behaviors, we can focus on relinquishing our desire to control an uncontrollable situation.

Interestingly, two of the guidelines Boss says are critical for coping—making meaning and finding new hope—are core to the story of the Christian faith. In John 10, Jesus paints a picture of belonging to the Good Shepherd, who will lay down his life for his sheep. Jesus, who is that Good Shepherd, knows us, sees us, and comes for us when we feel lost and alone. He calls us by name, and as we come to know the voice of Love, we are safely at home. This promise of God's with-ness sets the foundation for meaning-making and hope.

God's great love is particularly on display in Jesus's crucifixion and resurrection. Jesus was put to death on a cross on a Friday. He was exposed, ridiculed, and condemned. On Saturday, he rested in peace in a tomb. But when a couple of faithful women went to the tomb to tend to his body on Sunday, he was no longer there. God had raised him from the dead. God had exalted him, and he was with God, having received the promise of the Holy Spirit. Death does not have the final word in God's kingdom. What this means for us is that, when we're in the midst of suffering setbacks, wondering, and waiting, we can trust that God is present—that God is suffering with us and breaking into our pain. The assurance that death does not have the final word helps us *hope* for what might be and believe that new life is possible.

So much of life mirrors the resurrection arc God laid out thousands of years ago. When we experience challenges, change, and loss, we're living in the wake of Good Friday. When we're grieving what was and hoping for what might be, we're in the holding pattern of Holy Saturday. And when we experience new life sprouting on the heels of pain, we're invited by God to delight in the surprise and joy of Easter Sunday. These everyday moments when our work and our lives mirror the resurrection arc are known as *small r resurrection* moments.[17] They help us make meaning out of our grief.

Peace makes its way to us even though our boss is up to their same old tricks. Or, after a couple of anxious nights, we break loose in laughter on the phone with a friend. Perhaps we trade our usual nightcap for a cup of tea.

These are all small *r* resurrection moments. They're opportunities to see and experience God with us. They're chances to make meaning and find hope even as life is in flux.

Embracing grief work enables us to eventually welcome our dark emotions and befriend them. In this, like with any true friend, we are able to feel affection and gratitude for what grief brings us. Not for the loss, or even the pain. But for the love that lies underneath it and points us toward home. Inevitably, grief is a discovery process. Closure isn't the goal; hope is.

Letting go is the place of our ongoing conversion. The place where we declare through anguish and with hope, over and over again, that we cannot save ourselves.

Letting go is where grace meets us and tenderly welcomes us to give ourselves to the love of God found in Christ. We can trust that God meets us in our letting go because the story of Christ is one predicated on paradox.

That, in order to experience the hallelujah of Sunday, we must endure Friday's pain.

That joy knows sorrow.

That life is intertwined with death.

And that love always has the final word.

The Fruit of Letting Go

Several years ago, I started to become increasingly curious about what healthy, faithful, and fruitful leadership looked like. I had awoken to the person I did *not* want to be and was curious about who I *did* want to be. I was curious what healthy leadership looked like in the lives of others.

As this curiosity grew, it eventually became a research project housed at the Max De Pree Center for Leadership that I undertook with my colleague Dr. Meryl Herr. The findings were orienting and deeply encouraging. In the first round of research, we conducted eighteen focus groups where we asked people to use words or ideas that came to mind when they thought of healthy, faithful, and fruitful leaders. From early on, it was clear to Dr. Herr and me that this list was both beautiful and aspirational. Put simply, we were compiling a list of the leaders we longed to be. Turns out, I wasn't the only one who didn't have it all figured out.

Because Christian faith was foundational to these group discussions, the picture people constructed was one of discipleship. When we got to the exemplary interview round of research, I started to truly wonder, *Are we interviewing healthy world-class leaders? Or are we interviewing faithful disciples of Christ?* Not surprisingly, it was both.

These people had done remarkable work professionally. Led global companies through a financial crisis. Launched meaningful and useful products in the world. Made a measurable impact on the good of their community. Done business in a different, more wholehearted way. With that, they talked a lot about the difference Jesus made in both their lives and the way they led. In other words, they talked about the fruit Jesus produced in their lives and their leadership.

One of the more striking things Dr. Herr and I noticed was that the fruit of these people's leadership seemed to have something to do with their ability to embrace tough moments—crucible seasons, even—and grow through grief. The folks we interviewed embraced their own inner work when things got tough, and then, as time went on, they integrated their healing and growth into the way they led.[18]

But critically, it wasn't work they did alone.

This is seen in Lisa's story too. In order to get where she longed to go and produce good fruit along the way, she had to let go of the strategies that had worked so far and the stories she'd told herself for so long. Only she could let go; no one could do it for her. Still, she didn't try to do it alone. She had a support team and a community of people who loved her outside of her role at that organization and encouraged her in the hard work of letting go and going forward.

When we begin to let go, we open ourselves up to the good and holy work of observing ourselves in action, which inevitably leads to more letting go. In a sense, the fruit of letting go is more letting go. Sometimes old behaviors or habits come back to visit (especially when life feels like it's changing), and when they do, we can pause and redirect our energy to the new habit without judging or evaluating ourselves. Long-held habits, beliefs, and stories have a bit of a rubber band effect. It is natural and common to snap back to the old ways of being and doing, especially if we remain in many of the same environments.

As we release that which no longer is good, we will find that some people around us may not be very excited about the changes we are making—about the fruit of our growth. They may have a vested interest in things staying as they are. Doing our own inner work will inevitably make others look at themselves in new ways, and that's not necessarily comfortable. So, they may make attempts to drag us back into the patterns they are more comfortable with, even as we have worked to let them go.

Along the way, it is both tempting and inevitable we will do some going back to old ways, both because patterns are usually deeply ingrained and because we want to preserve friendships. But, in this temptation to lean on old patterns, there is also the invitation to see if a new way is possible. We begin to take small steps into this new possibility, even if we can't clearly see where it will lead us. In order to see if new ways are possible—whether within a system, with people, or just in ourselves—we have to step headfirst into the unknown.

We have to let go and move forward even when everything keeps changing.

A Prayer for When
I'm White-Knuckling It

Gracious God,
one who holds out a hand when my fists are clenched,
help me to pause and breathe and notice.

Help me to trust that you are with me
even when I
am afraid
unsure
confused
discouraged
hopeless.

As my breathing gets deeper
and my fists start to unclench,
I let the stories I've told myself for so long fall away.
I let the have-tos and the shoulds of yesterday not be
    the promises of tomorrow.
I let go of my need to control and admit to you, God,
    that I feel afraid.

Hands now open, I realize I'm on unstable ground.
Guide me as my legs shake,
as I learn to walk in the fog.

Bless you, God.
You promise to be with me wherever I go.
May your presence be the source of my courage to
    keep letting go.

Amen.

Embrace the
Unfiguroutable

Starting very young, many of us learn that we are rewarded for having the right answers.[1] The right answer in class warrants verbal praise from our teacher. At school, with friends, and at home, we're celebrated for knowing the answers to whatever problem is put in front of us. Being celebrated for figuring it out shapes our self-identity. It forms us into people who feel most comfortable when we have the right answer or *know what to do*.[2]

Now, this isn't all bad. In this pursuit of knowledge, we learn how to solve actual problems. But having the right answers will take us only so far. It may work well as kids, but as we grow, we inevitably come up against moments where our problem-solving skills don't yield the answers we're hoping for.

In a rapidly changing world, the answers are less static. The fog sets in more regularly, and quick solutions are not truly helpful, especially if whatever season we find ourselves in has woken us up to notice what is not working in our own lives or made us aware that we want to go somewhere new. This kind of clarity usually brings about more disorientation. Sure, we have clarity about the basic direction we're headed, but we cannot see the path to get there. The same answers that work on a sunny day won't navigate us out of the fog. What will? Well, this is where it gets challenging. Some disorientation just isn't solvable. Some problems don't have answers at all, especially when the world as we know it is in flux.

Some things are just simply unfiguroutable.

The fog doesn't always lift, but that doesn't mean we can't make our way through it. Even when there are more problems to solve and no right answers in sight. We have to make the conscious choice to step further into the fog, acknowledging that we don't know what to do next but are curious about what lies ahead.

NAVIGATIONAL SKILL #4:

Embrace the Unfiguroutable

As I recognize I don't actually know what to do, I shift from problem-solving to curiosity.

Somewhere New

Meet Alice. Alice is a senior leader in a fast-growing technology company. She worked hard to establish herself as the go-to expert on one of the company's most sought-after products. She was so good at her job that senior leadership offered her a big, fancy promotion. Instead of being an in-house expert, she would have a client-facing role. The promotion came with a lot more money, which was good because she and her husband were trying to buy a house. The job also came with more autonomy and a flexible work schedule, both of which were also attractive to Alice.

Great news, right? Not so fast.

Alice describes herself as a woman who likes to have a plan. She's most comfortable when she's in the problem-solving seat on complex, product-related issues. She is quite skilled at gathering, storing, and sorting through an incredible amount of information quickly and reliably. But, in her new role, she was now in charge of business development for the product she was an expert on. Her new job was to help prospective clients and existing ones feel good about working with her company by getting them comfortable with the product.

While she knew that relating to customers would be about much more than product knowledge, she underestimated the number of situations she'd be in for which she did not have the answers.

When will that technical issue be resolved?

Why aren't my issues being treated with priority?

What can you do to fix this?

These kinds of questions were not usually answerable, at least not quickly. That meant managing the client relationship required a kind of diplomacy and savvy that Alice just did not come by naturally.

She felt really anxious about all the not knowing. She started to withdraw from not only her clients but her colleagues too. She found herself longing for the days when everyone came to her for the answers. She wondered if she was cut out for this kind of role. She considered trying to get her old job back, even if it meant a big pay cut and looking like a complete failure. Alice had never failed at this level before and certainly not with so many people watching. She'd never been here before, and she wasn't quite sure where she wanted to go next.

In this new position with these new problems, she just didn't have the answers to any of it.

> **COMMON POSTURE:** It's my job to figure it out now and know what to do.
>
> **UNCOMMON POSTURE:** Greater learning emerges when I can step back, gain perspective, and seek wise ground to stand on.

Sometimes we just don't know what to do. We don't have the answers for the problems we want to solve. Should Alice try to grow into her new job? Get her old one back? Leave the company? It's hard to tell. Any quick decision could end up being the wrong one. Maybe there's no right or wrong answer at all!

With that in mind, the question becomes, How do we know what to do when we don't know what to do?

Life's Threshold Moments

There comes a time where we have to press further into the unfiguroutable in order to get clear. That means we have to get comfortable living in a kind of in-between space. The space that feels like we're suspended in motion, upside down and without a sense of which way to go.

Think back to the caterpillar on the precipice of becoming a butterfly. After days of eating and growing, a caterpillar seems to know it's time to shed its skin one last time and transition to its chrysalis. It knows it's time to make its way into the unknown. After it disappears inside its chrysalis, it might seem as if nothing much is happening inside. But the caterpillar has entered the in-between—a threshold space. It is no longer a caterpillar but not yet a butterfly.

This threshold space is vital for us in a similar way. It's where we begin to let go of the old and prepare for the new—to, in a sense, stand between two realities. This is perhaps most obvious when we face overt moments of transition in our lives—new jobs, the death of someone we love, living in a new city. But it's even more true in our own becoming. For Alice, it was the space between realizing something had to change but not yet knowing exactly what it was, much less how to get there.

For Stew, it was different. Stew was a brand-new manager, and his only direct report was causing him all kinds of stress. He suspected that the employee needed a kind of care that he as a manager could not offer and that the small family business they both worked for was not equipped to provide. Stew and I emailed every so often, mostly me checking in on his situation. One day his response surprised me.

"Not much has changed," he wrote, "but I am changing, and I suppose that makes all the difference."

In the in-between—in the flux and fog—Stew was growing. And the same can be true for us all! If we accept that what got us to where we are won't get us to where we want to go, and we trust that by pressing deeper into the unknown we can learn and grow, we'll begin to figure out a way forward.

Remember, in the chrysalis, the elements needed for the adult butterfly to emerge are not present in the biological makeup of the caterpillar. In fact, of the two kinds of cells the caterpillar brings into the chrysalis, one must get completely consumed by the other in order to make way for the butterfly. Which means that this kind of change is not a simple layering of new things, behavior, mindsets, or even values onto the old. Instead, it's a transformation from one thing to another.

When Paul writes to the church at Philippi, he describes Jesus's own emptying of divine power in order that he might become fully human in this world. Paul encourages the church to have this same kind of mindset as they relate to one another: "[Jesus] made himself nothing by taking the very nature of a servant, being made in human likeness. And being found in appearance as a man, he humbled himself by becoming obedient to death—even death on a cross" (Phil. 2:7–8).

By embracing the unfiguroutable, we get a sense of what needs to die before there is any clarity about what might come next. Our egos, coping mechanisms, limiting narratives others have put on us, harmful patterns of relating to others, a vision of our lives we had for ourselves—it all may have to be given up in order for us to emerge as someone changed, someone new.

This march into the unknown happens by taking next doable risk after next doable risk.

When my husband and I first started wondering about whether we might move from Los Angeles to the Midwest with our two small kids, we quite literally couldn't see ourselves anywhere other than LA. We met and fell in love there. We started our careers there. It's where we bought our first house and brought our babies home from the hospital. In nearly every way, LA was home.

It took us three years to finally make the decision to move. There was a lot of talking and a lot of tears. Truth be told, there was some fighting too. Could we really be Midwesterners? How would we do with winter? (Spoiler alert: not great.) For me, the real crux of it all boiled down to one thing: Could I come full circle to the place I had declared I would never return to?

This question was one I eventually came to realize I could not figure out in my own head, in conversations with my husband, or even with family and friends. It was a question I could only answer by stepping into the in-between and giving it a try.

At first, my husband wasn't ready to go. We spent two years talking through it until he was ready to make the leap. Then, one day, he came to me and told me he was, without a shadow of a doubt, excited to go. As it turned out, the possibility made real was too much for me to handle. A whole new bout of pain and wondering surfaced, and I told him I just wasn't ready to leave LA. My next doable risk was different than I would have imagined. So we took another year before finally making the move.

What I remember from very early on in our conversations was that I knew we had left one place and were not quite to another. We were neither here nor there but somewhere in between. We were physically in one place but mentally and emotionally living in the unknown.

When I think back on those years, I remember them as one giant in-between. We were in an extended season of liminality.

Liminality is a word scholars use to refer to the in-between space—the place of being neither here nor there. It is the tension in the middle. It is simultaneously embracing the gateway to the next thing while allowing ourselves to linger in and learn from what we're leaving behind. To say that life is in flux is to say that we live amid near-constant liminality.

In other words, all of us bump up against threshold moments all the time. It happens in the big, individual decisions like *Should I try to get my job back?* or *Should we make this move?* but also in things like the transfer of power from generation to generation or the looming impacts of climate change. Life in flux is inherently full of unfiguroutable realities, seasons, and moments.

In so many ways, this is where the real work begins. When the place of our own waking up and letting go leads us to the edge of the space we know, the way forward is both terrifying and promising. Richard Rohr says, "We must leave business as usual—which often looks like a sleepwalking trance through daily life if we are not conscious—and voluntarily enter a world where the rules and expectations are quite different."[3] Walking head-on into the unfiguroutable is the way home amid life in flux.

How to Actually Embrace the Unknown

COMMON POSTURE: I am a problem solver. I'll just double down until I get to the answer.

UNCOMMON POSTURE: I don't know. Let's get on the pathway to unlearning and relearning.

Unfiguroutable spaces are still uncomfortable. Why? Because they are ambiguous. They're messy, they're risky, and they can't be controlled. Even if we trust God can and will find us in the unknown, the reality of facing that which we cannot see clearly is difficult.

It's natural to long for resolution when tension is present. However, it's in the tension that growth and learning occur, so resolving it too quickly (or sometimes even at all!) won't take us where we want to go.

Let's take the common tension of work/life balance as an example. Many people express a tension between their work lives and their family lives. One puts pressure on the other. Any quick attempt to resolve this tension ends in dichotomy. If we choose our family and quit our job, we won't have the means to pay for our family's needs. If we go all in on work, we neglect our family. To find this elusive sense of balance, we have to be willing to move slowly, intentionally, and even uncomfortably toward an answer. There can be no quick fixes in the unknown! Learning to live in healthy tension and ambiguity is part of the maturing and growing that happen when we allow ourselves to embrace the unknown.

Toward helping us exist in the tension and withstand ambiguity and uncertainty, Lisa and I have created a set of four somewhat paradoxical principles. These are not at all meant to be quick how-tos for the unknown (because, remember, those don't exist). Instead, they offer some guardrails for the way forward.

1. Interrogate what is known, but also, trust ourselves.

One of the hardest parts of learning to embrace the unfig-uroutable is that we must learn to make new types of decisions. As we learn to pause and step back, we are quite literally learning to halt our decision-making processes—the very skills we've relied on for so long. The more well-versed we are in problem-solving, the more unlearning and relearning we'll have to do.

Experts from a variety of fields have useful paradigms for this process, but one of the seminal frameworks comes from adult learning expert Jack Mezirow. In education and business circles alike, he's made popular the idea of *transformative learning*, which outlines how adults unlearn and relearn. At the heart of his work is the idea that, in order for adults to grow and learn, we have to be able to critically evaluate our values, assumptions, and beliefs. Oftentimes, we only do this kind of critical reflection when there is some sort of an inciting incident.[4] An inciting incident might come in the form of one of the transitions we undergo every twelve to eighteen months. Or it may be any number of volatile catastrophes we bear witness to in our communities or around the world. When disruption happens and disorientation sets in, the seedlings of growth are planted. If we're surrounded by people who love us and point us toward figuring out a new way forward, we can leverage these inciting incidents (again, think pain or possibility) to uncover what we believe, face our own shadows, consider how and why we relate to others the way we do, and eventually experiment with new decision-making patterns. The evidence from adult learning is persuasive: we can, in fact, unlearn and relearn.

Take James, who was in advertising. He was extremely creative and full of great ideas, but he also had a bad habit of interrupting other people. So much so that his colleagues eventually stopped inviting him to informal brainstorming meetings, and they were bold enough to be honest about why. As a result, he found himself out of the loop on some of the company's key projects and relegated to smaller projects he could do by himself.

When James complained to his wife, she confirmed for him that he did interrupt people too often. At first, James was defensive. He felt like his wife didn't have his back. But he also didn't like being relegated to smaller accounts and didn't have a clue of how to get back in with his teammates except to work on this issue. So, he decided to try to break his bad behavior.

This marked a long season of flux for James, one in which he had to get curious about things he'd rather avoid.

Because he didn't know how to break his habit, James enlisted a mentor to help him make an action plan. When the mentor asked him *why* he interrupted so much, James found himself with nothing to say. He didn't know why he interrupted; that part, to him, was the unknown. His mentor encouraged him to get direct feedback from each of his colleagues over Zoom—so that he could mute himself and not accidentally talk over anyone in the process. His mentor warned him that what he heard might be painful, so he'd need to make space in his day to process the calls.

With the encouragement of his mentor behind him, James asked for fifteen-minute calls back-to-back with four different people on his team. On them, he asked just one question before hitting mute: "Why do you think I interrupt?"

Every single one of his colleagues said a version of the same thing: "You seem to need to be the smartest person in the room. You think your ideas are better than ours. You say you like working with us, but your actions show that you're not really a team player at all."

On the first call, James felt defensive. *What do they know, anyway?* In the second, however, he was surprised. By the third, he was wincing in pain, and after the fourth, he was in tears. James experienced the feedback as incredibly disorienting. With each call, more fog settled in. How was it that he was so out of touch with everyone else's sense of who he was? How might he go about unlearning this old way and relearning a new, unknown way?

As a result of the feedback from his colleagues, James had to decide how much he was willing to interrogate and break down his interrupting. This was another threshold moment. He had to decide if he would enter willingly into the liminality of not being completely sure about who he was if he was not the smartest person in the room.

James had a shadow side. We all do. It is the part of who we are that we cannot see. Like a physical shadow, it is always behind us, just out of view. Richard Rohr describes our shadow kind of like a stage mask we put on and take off. The masks we wear aren't necessarily bad or evil. Sometimes we don't even know we're putting one on. But the masks hide our truest selves. Sometimes we work very hard to hide what we don't want others to see. [5] The more we have crafted an idealized mask (or role or persona) to show the world, the deeper we will have to go to uncover the trueness of who we are. Oof.

When we interrogate our own assumptions, chances are our feelings of disorientation and discomfort will only grow. Not only is this place of unlearning a place where we're examining deeply held beliefs, it's a space where we're facing the shadow parts of ourselves, potentially for the first time.

Because the world is in such flux, and disruption is around every corner, being able to uncover our shadows and change our minds (especially about ourselves!) and our behavior is one of the most important skills in our modern age. Organizational psychologist Adam Grant says it this way: "Intelligence is traditionally viewed as the ability to think and learn. Yet in a turbulent world, there's another set of cognitive skills that might matter more: the ability to rethink and unlearn."[6]

What's critical to grasp here is that, as we do this, it's not the kind of interrogation that discounts or demeans our innermost longings or who we are as people. Remember, those longings can point our way home. We can trust ourselves deep down, even when we're confronting our shadow and changing our mind about ourselves. This is an interrogation designed to help us see what we haven't seen before and calibrate a new course forward based on what we may need to unlearn and relearn to get there.

When I've found myself unhappy in work environments, I've had to stop and get honest in my own interrogation of myself. Like James, I took the advice of a mentor and started to work on myself, but I really didn't know what parts of myself I could trust going forward.

There is a psychological concept called *locus of control*, which has to do with how we perceive our own agency in affecting change in our own lives. Our locus of control can be internal or external. Author and psychologist Alison Cook writes,

> When you have an internal locus of control, you tend to look to resources within yourself—including God's Spirit—to affect change, make decisions, and create impact. In contrast, when you lean towards an external locus of control, you tend to view what happens to you as outside of your control.[7]

Cook goes on to describe the differences in how society conditions people. For example, men are conditioned toward an internal locus of control, while women are conditioned toward an external one. The problem is, as Cook writes, "An internal locus of control relates to higher levels of confidence and improved mental health, while an external locus of control tends to correlate with increased feelings of anxiety and depression."[8]

For some of us, we have to relearn or learn for the first time how to trust ourselves. This gets complicated if it happens alongside facing shadow parts of ourselves.

More fog.

More cutting the engine and listening for signals.

More letting go.

Trusting ourselves is fundamentally about believing our own goodness and committing to be kind and respectful to ourselves regardless of what we learn about ourselves or how much fog we're in. Of course, asking the right questions and trusting our answers isn't easy. So, for the days when trusting ourselves just feels like it's too far-fetched, we can fall back on this: God can be trusted to meet us in our pain. With the psalmist, we sing, "The LORD is near to the brokenhearted and saves the crushed in spirit" (Ps. 34:18 NRSVUE).

Yes, God's loving presence is a powerful sustainer in the midst of the unfiguroutable. When we can't seem to trust ourselves, we can certainly trust that!

2. Look back to go forward.

In practical theology, there is a framework for thinking about the movement between values and actions. The basic idea is that the deepest beliefs we hold inform our actions at every turn—even when we can't see them or haven't articulated those commitments. No action is without a system of beliefs driving it. What this also means is that, in order to consider what kind of actions we want to take in the future, we have to be willing to look back and reflect on both our actions of the past and what these actions reveal about our beliefs.[9] Sometimes when we do this, we find gaps between what we say we believe and what our actions reveal we believe.

Let's keep looking at James's story here. Before James heard from his colleagues, he would have told you he valued communication, teamwork, and brainstorming sessions that generate the most creative ideas. But when faced with what others had to say about him, it looked like his beliefs in action were quite different. His actions showed that he valued communicating his ideas and that he believed he should be the star player on any team. He did believe in brainstorming sessions that generate the most creative ideas, but he also believed he was often the one with those ideas.

Mezirow helps us understand that in order to make new sense of old experiences, "We reinterpret an old experience (or a new one) from a new set of expectations, thus giving a new meaning and perspective to the old experience."[10]

Feeling completely bewildered by the fact that his actions were so out of sync with what he said he believed, James had a decision to make. Was he willing to walk into a different kind of in-between space? One in which he would have to work to interrogate his deeply held beliefs? One in which he would have to work to figure out what felt unfiguroutable in him?

In all this, the work of remembering is critical. The early chapters of the book of Joshua are particularly helpful here. The book starts with a transition—an ending, really: "Moses my servant is dead" (Josh. 1:2).

Based on this, God tells Joshua to get all the Israelites across the Jordan River into the land that God is about to give to them. Joshua is given very specific instructions on what to do, and God is very clear: "As I was with Moses, so I will be with you; I will never leave you nor forsake you" (v. 5).

God's promise to be with Joshua is rooted in the remembrance of God's presence with Moses. It's from that promise of God's presence that Joshua is told, "Be strong and courageous, because you will lead these people to inherit the land I swore to their ancestors to give them" (v. 6).

As the next few chapters progress, we see the assurance of God's presence come to life. We also see Joshua's step-by-step obedience in response. God guides and Joshua responds. Along the way, God continues to acknowledge just how scary the unknown is, offering Joshua regular encouragement. Because of God's past and present faithfulness, Joshua doesn't have to move forward from a place of fear. Instead, he can go from a place of courage. Joshua does not know what awaits him along the way, but the Lord guides his steps.

The entire book of Joshua represents a threshold season for the people of Israel as they move out of exile and into the land that had been promised to them. So much unknown, so much unfiguroutable. Joshua helps the people make their way forward by looking back and remembering what God had already done and using those fulfilled promises as a source of courage for the way forward.

To take life one step at a time, to look back and go forward, often means releasing outcomes, plans, and strategy. Joshua had to do it in order to follow God's leading in his life. Our friend James was going to need to do it in order to get to the root of what was causing his behavior and disconnect at work. And when our lives are in flux, we may find ourselves in the same position. When we do, we can trust that God is with us and for us, guiding us as we look back to go forward, deeper into the unknown.

3. Expect the heat to rise. Learn how to stay in the kitchen.

This work of facing hard things can truly happen only when we feel safe enough to confront our deeply held assumptions while challenged enough that we're motivated to actually change. Organizational scholars Ronald Heifetz and Marty Linsky call this kind of space a *holding environment*.[11] Holding environments are intentionally created safe spaces where we are valued and challenged. They come in all shapes and sizes, but because they're intangible, they're not always easy to spot. For example, we might see a counselor or a coach who helps create a holding environment. Or our boss might help create one. Our parent might have created one for us as a child or even now as an adult. Some learning environments can also act as holding environments—especially ones designed for transformation. No matter the space, these holding environments are key to navigating life in flux in productive ways.

Consider when in the past you've felt safe enough to wrestle with deeply held assumptions but also motivated to grow or change. For most of us, it's not a common experience. Maybe you've experienced this with a mentor or a partner, a counselor, a teacher, or even a group of people like a church or a class. If you can think of this type of space, consider what made that space (metaphorical or physical) feel safe. Consider what made it feel like the right kind of challenging. Maybe it's the same space where you don't have to think about being yourself, but you also know people are going to call you out on your stuff. Maybe it's with the sister who has always known you or the best friend who takes your hand as life takes you into the valley.

One of the key aspects of a holding environment is metaphorical heat. Picture a thermostat setting the temperature of the space. Things have to be cool enough that we can withstand the process of interrogating ourselves and reflecting on the past but warm enough that we are actually motivated toward change as we look toward the future. The temperature isn't fixed. An effective holding environment dials the thermostat up to prompt change and dials it down when we feel too anxious or overwhelmed.

Heifetz and Linsky's work is about equipping leaders in systems to learn to adjust the thermostat for the sake of change, but here, we want to build off and broaden it so that we can begin to recognize what makes the heat rise and fall as we're making our individual way through the unfiguroutable. As we navigate life in flux, the world is dialing up the heat. That means we need to recognize when things feel hotter and know what to focus on if we need to dial down the temperature.

Heat is turned up when:

We can't resolve ambiguity.

Tough questions rise to the top.

The reality of what we discover is too painful.

Conflict is center stage.

Heat is turned down when:

We focus on small, doable aspects of change.

We establish a clear process for ambiguous work.

We temporarily step out of the mess.

We slow down.

Let's go back to James. Being uninvited to brainstorming meetings turned up the heat. Working with a mentor to identify four safe people and solicit feedback in small, digestible bits helped him lower the heat. Then, the feedback he got made the heat go way up, both because he felt the conflict of the relationships and because of the pain of what his colleagues were saying. From there, James started to have intentional conversations with his wife, friends, and therapist. Those sometimes brought the heat down, but they mostly kept it high—high enough to feel motivation but not so high that he felt like he needed to "leave the kitchen."

After a few months of James working through this on his own, his wife suggested he ask his colleagues if he could come back to the meetings on a trial period. The condition? He would commit to not talking at all. They agreed.

A risk for him.

A risk for them.

Raising the heat for all.

His colleagues never had it out for James; they just had to set their own boundaries. Being welcomed back into the group, even if he was silent, turned the heat way down for James. It gave him something practical he could accomplish even while he was sorting through his larger questions of identity and belief.

When the fog sets in, it's hard to just sit in it. Especially if we find that, like James, we're part of the problem. This isn't to say that there aren't situations where the problem is someone else's. Inappropriate bosses, toxic friends, and difficult partners—sometimes truly disorienting situations have nothing to do with the natural flux of life and everything to do with people's deeply ingrained and destructive habits.

In an increasingly complex world in which personal transitions are layered on top of systemic disruptions that don't have clear or known solutions, there is less and less we can reliably plan and execute. The world is speeding up every day! In light of all this, let's develop the capacity to recognize the temperature of any given environment so that we might feel more at ease in the inevitable flux of the world.

4. Growth happens when we remain (in Jesus).

Jesus says this: "Remain in me, as I also remain in you. No branch can bear fruit by itself; it must remain in the vine. Neither can you bear fruit unless you remain in me" (John 15:4).

It is as simple and as complicated as that. In an increasingly disrupted and disoriented world, in order for our lives to bear the fruit we imagine is possible, we must *remain* rooted in what orients us deep down. In this, we acknowledge and live as though Christ already remains, or "dwells," in us.

It's kind of an odd thing to say, isn't it? That in the midst of a changing world in which there is so much work to do and so much to look at within ourselves, we must *remain*. It might feel counterintuitive to think about settling in and staying put when everything seems to be accelerating. Now, let me be clear: this passage doesn't say we need to remain stuck in old ways. It doesn't caution against exploration or taking new paths. Rather, it gives us an anchor in the midst of unpredictability. Though the storms may come and the seasons may change, the vine promises to be there for the branches.

In the winter, when a vine is dormant, it almost looks dead, lying gnarly and twisted. The older the vine, the more twisted and gnarly it appears. To the inexperienced eye, it might look like something that should be pulled out or eradicated. But that would be a mistake. The vine is doing critical work in its fallow state, digging its roots deeper into the ground and seeking richer nutrients that will produce better fruit.

When the spring comes and the vines begin to blossom and produce fruit, the vintner will walk the rows of vines and prune them with a practiced eye, clipping off early fruit that is of lesser quality to allow the better fruit to draw the water and nutrition needed to produce lush, vibrant grapes. Our own formation is much like this. Going deeper with God in times of uncertainty allows our roots to be strengthened, and eventually we grow and are pruned so that, over time, we can become more and more fruitful too.

Because so much has and will continue to change, Lisa and I have come to recognize this place of *remaining* as a steady source of life through disruption. It helps as we discern what types of work we're fit for, what our gifts are, and how we might learn from others. It's certainly an anchor point for making sense of the whole idea of calling. Over time, just as branches are formed by water, sun, and soil, we are formed by the ways of Jesus, other people, our work, and all that's happening around us. It's comforting, actually, that over and over in Scripture, God's most central call to us is one of being before doing. One of belonging before working. One where life on the vine precedes any fruitfulness.

Think back to Alice, whom we met at the start of this chapter. After a few months in her new role, she realized that the amount of ambiguity required for her to operate daily was just too stressful. Not only was she filled with anxiety, she was also bringing anxiety to the team and the clients in ways that were not good for anyone. When a lateral position opened up in another business unit—one that required her to become a deep subject matter expert on a couple of key product areas—she had good conversations with both her direct boss and the executive leader of her existing team. They both supported her fully in applying for the new role, which she was awarded. A few years later, she continues to excel in that new position. In fact, she describes it as the best job she's ever had! But it came after about a year of professional flux—a season of lots of unknowns. She got to where she wanted to be after a lot of wondering and wrestling.

She got there by taking one small step at a time into the unknown.

Sometimes we are thrust into disorientation by involuntary events, and sometimes by decisions we've made. Regardless, it's difficult to make the conscious choice in the midst of the fog to step back and sit with hard questions amid the pressures of daily living. To acknowledge that we so often stand on the threshold between what is and what might be. To recognize that we're often trying to figure out the unfiguroutable. But creating space for this effort, with support from a community of trusted guides, is essential to our pursuit of making our way forward amid a life in flux.

A Prayer for When
I Want to Problem-Solve

Oh, Lord, here I am . . . again,
exerting all my energy to solve the latest problem,
rescue the latest relationship,
and fix what needs to be fixed.

And it is NOT working.
The problem just isn't clear . . . so I cannot fix it.
The relationship is not mine to save, and yet I keep
    showing up with my solutions.
The thing that needs fixing seems just irreparable.

All my wits, my strength, my skills are just not enough.
And how I hate that . . .

But with my head down,
huffing and puffing,
straining and pushing,
I know I am missing
something important.

And so I lift up my head, stretch out my back, and shift
    my gaze.
And slowly, bit by bit, I shift.

Open my mind,
make me curious.
Help me welcome the not knowing,
the unfiguroutable.

Amen.

Set Your Compass

Sean spent the better part of a decade building a division of a large, public university. He'd been charged by a series of advisers to take the work he was doing further by spearheading a major change effort. But as he dug in to do the hard work of change, the same advisers and mentors who'd encouraged this path turned against him—inexplicably and quite dramatically.

Unanswered emails. Brush-offs in meetings. Lunches without him.

As he felt pushed further and further away from decision-making, Sean felt he had no choice but to resign. He did so as his leadership and his character were being questioned. He was heartbroken. His world had been turned upside down.

He was at the start of what he would later describe as a full-on identity crisis. Because he had defined himself by his work and its relationships, he had no clear picture of who he was apart from this role and the expectations others had for him. Now he found himself at a crossroads. Should he double down on all that had gotten him to where he was? Or release what he'd spent his career working toward for a new path forward? Talk about a life in flux. The fog had settled over Sean, quickly and dramatically.

To navigate forward, he'd need a new skill.

NAVIGATIONAL SKILL #5:
Set Your Compass

I recover my ability to embrace God's loving call as True North.

Before that foggy day in Maine, young Roger had cultivated a lot of skills for staying safe on the water. He needed every one of them to navigate his way to safety. But he was missing one important tool that would have made the journey less arduous and less frightening: a compass.

The rapid pace and constant disorientation of today's world reveal that, more often than not, we are also without a compass. When the fog settles in and we aren't sure where to go next, we need a guiding force pointing to our True North. Because disruption is by nature unannounced and therefore disorienting, it's hard to navigate our way through it without a sense of direction.

So, the deeper question becomes, Have we cultivated an understanding of our own True North?

As people of faith, our True North is found in God. Knowing and experiencing God's loving calling is the guide that beckons us toward our deepest sense of home. When we're in the thick of it, we trust that God's love is stable, safe, expansive, and good. God is both with us in our disorientation and also out in front of us, calling us forward.

The Concept of Calling

One way to think about how we respond to God's love—how we might make our way in this work of navigating flux—is through the theological concept of *calling*.

Calling is a difficult concept. I meet a lot of people for whom the whole notion is a mixed bag. For some, it's an attractive idea—one that conjures up images of how God speaks to us and helps us know what is ours to do. For others, calling is an idea that has more baggage—a theological word that has been misused to signal privilege or spiritual specialness. Lisa and I have observed that it's common for people to think about calling as something "out there"—something external to us that we need to go and find (remember the locus of control!).

Calling is a job I love.

Calling is the special thing I was made to do.

Calling is the work I can't not do.

To limit the idea of God's calling to professional work or one special thing is to miss the wider picture of what God is doing in the world. God's loving call is much bigger than an economic system or an individual's career path. It's not just a way for us privileged folks to search out our own significance through our passions. Plus, if calling is something to be found *out there*, it sets up the expectation that our work is to *go after it.* Cue overfunctioning and busying ourselves in an effort to meet the expectations others have put on us.

Most of us do not get a single call from God that manifests itself in a singular job that we then spend our lives responding to. God is much more dynamic than that. Calling is an ongoing conversation—a constant call and response. It is a life of followership. It is a path of discovery. And it's about so much more than work!

Hearing and responding to God's callings is an inside out process. It's more excavation than treasure hunting.[1] It happens little by little, not all at once. Ultimately, it's about connecting with the divine imprinted on us and letting that align us with God's loving, just, and gracious activity in the world. When we're awake to our own lives, doing the worthy work of unclenching our white-knuckled fists and welcoming what the fog has to teach us, we naturally start to open ourselves up to hear the foghorns and bell buoys that call us home.

Then, calling becomes a compass.

> **COMMON POSTURE:** Calling is about a career, occupation, or my passion.
>
> **UNCOMMON POSTURE:** Calling is about listening for and responding to the One who calls me to belong in every part of life.

Any ambivalence we might have about the whole idea of calling only gets heightened when we can't see more than an arm's length ahead in our own lives. When we're unsure of who we are, where we belong, or what in the world we're supposed to be doing, we crave calling to help us figure it out. Once we've truly woken up to what's not working and started to let go of the stories and strategies we're holding on to, it takes a while to adjust to the truth. Things often get much foggier before they get clearer. Eventually, that clarity will come by going through, not around, the unfiguroutable.

When we feel like we can't stand how much life is changing, God can be trusted to guide us in flux. Unlike us, God is not disoriented or confused about who we are or the way forward.

God is with us in the fog.

God is calling us home.

With that in mind, let's start to craft a bigger, ultimately more grounding, and hopeful picture of what calling looks like by studying a few concepts found in Scripture.

If We Have Callings, We Have a Caller

We can't have a calling without a Caller.[2] Because calling comes from the same place it leads us to, we can understand that God is the One who calls us. But what does it sound like to be called by God?

We see God calling in somewhat dramatic fashion when God calls Moses to come near a burning bush. "When the LORD saw that he had gone over to look, God called to him from within the bush, 'Moses! Moses!'" (Exod. 3:4).

Or how about when God calls Samuel while the boy is fast asleep in the middle of the night? "Then the LORD called, 'Samuel! Samuel!' and he said, 'Here I am!'" (1 Sam. 3:4 NRSVUE).

Equally as dramatic is when, near Damascus, Saul encounters a bright flash and the voice of Jesus condemning him for persecuting people. He changes his name to Paul, signifying the transforming power of encountering God.[3]

Of course, God doesn't always talk to us through a burning bush, wake us up in the middle of the night in a dream, or use lightning while we're out on a walk. In fact, that's not how it usually feels at all! Yes, sometimes, some of us hear from God clearly, but often God's guidance feels more abstract, like a light in a dark space, or the honest cracking open of pain, or a cool breeze that touches our cheeks.

Many times, God speaks through people. Henry Cloud describes people as "God's plan A" for our growth and maturing.[4] While we are waiting for the burning bush, God has placed people in our lives who help us hear from God. Even as Paul greets the Corinthian church in his first letter to them, he points toward his relationship with Sosthenes. Consider Esther as well. It was her uncle Mordecai who spoke through one of the king's servants to call Esther to advocate for her people. And, of course, God called Mary to be the mother of Jesus through an angel. In the pages of Scripture, we see over and over again God's plan A at work.

Let's look at the story of Samuel when he first hears from God, for example. This is one of my favorite stories in the Bible because it's about the type of unlearning and relearning we've talked about. It's about embracing the unfiguroutable and making our way deeper into the fog. It's a real-life example of setting our compass toward our calling from God.

Samuel is traveling with his mentor, Eli. The story picks up in the middle of the night when both are fast asleep. God calls out to Samuel by name. When Samuel hears his name, he hops up and runs over to Eli, ready to help him with whatever he needs. But Eli did not call for Samuel. So Samuel goes back to bed. Again, God calls Samuel, and again, Samuel goes to Eli. It isn't until the third time that Eli realizes it must be the Lord who is calling Samuel. He tells Samuel that the next time the boy hears the voice of the Lord, to respond that he's listening.

Samuel quite literally doesn't recognize the voice of God. And, if we're honest, I think that's true for us too. Even if we're not hearing God talk in an audible way, it can be easy to miss the signs God is speaking to us. We need mentors and friends who have walked the path and can sit with us patiently to help us attune to God. We need people who can help us learn to pay attention and sit in the unknown and eventually notice what we can't see on our own.

The call of God often comes through other people. Critically, what we hear from others must align with our internal sense of belonging. Other people don't get to put their agendas on us and say that God told them to say those things. But we also want to make the space to hear genuinely from trusted friends and guides (even stuff that might be hard for us to hear).

Nesting Dolls

In the fog, it's often hard to hear God's calling, both collectively and individually. That's why we need the skills to navigate toward it. We need to find a way to set our compass toward that sense of True North.

Because calling sometimes feels so confusing, it has been helpful for me to think about calling as a set of nesting dolls, in that there are layers of calling that come together to make a whole.[5] We'll start at the innermost doll, working from there to add layers until we get to our particular calling. This means whatever particular places, roles, or work God has called you to are a context in which you can respond to all that's nested within.

Let's take a minute to unpack those layers together.

1. Innermost doll: God calls us to belong.

Calling is most centrally about belonging to God and being "belongers" wherever we are, whomever we're with, and whatever we're doing. Belonging to God carries with it an aura of abundance. Jesus says, "I have come that they may have life, and have it to the full" (John 10:10). Here, Jesus is portrayed as the Good Shepherd, lovingly and powerfully watching out for his sheep so that they might have life to the fullest. About us, the belonging sheep, Jesus adds, "My sheep hear my voice. I know them, and they follow me. I give them eternal life, and they will never perish. No one will snatch them out of my hand" (vv. 27–28 NRSVUE).

The sheep hear God's voice. When we listen and follow it, we can be secure in the God who is leading us. No one can snatch us from the Shepherd's hand. No one will leave us stranded in the fog.

As you consider the different times you've sensed God calling you, it's important to remember that calling is about more than just you. Yes, God calls individuals, but God doesn't call only individuals. God also calls people together in community. Why? Because community matters.

In addressing the Corinthian believers, Paul says, "To the church of God that is in Corinth, to those who are sanctified in

Christ Jesus, called to be saints, together with all those who in every place call on the name of our Lord Jesus Christ, both their Lord and ours" (1 Cor. 1:2 NRSVUE).

Together, the church—the people of God—are called to the work of God in this world.

Yes, this call from God is both an individual and a collective call. While it's wholly ours to own, it's not just ours to own. The fullness of this call comes to life in the presence of community. When we respond to God's summons to belong, we are grafted into a family of sisters and brothers who, like us, are also made to belong. In this, our sense of calling to belong to God comes to vivid life in the context of others.

Though we are called singularly by God, our sense of calling takes shape among and with the community that has formed us. Practical theologian Dr. Patrick Reyes says that, because we are formed by and with others, calling is always contextual, auto-biographical, and communal.[6] Belonging shapes what we believe deep down inside. And because context varies widely, so do our perceptions about what and who we're called to.

Of course, not all contexts are the same. In his book *The Purpose Gap*, Reyes writes, "The dominant culture's vocational literature completely disregards place and community. [But] finding and pursuing purpose is not a linear or spatially inconsequential endeavor."[7] I am a white woman born into a middle-class family in the American Midwest, so from an early age that shaped my sense of what was possible. Whether anyone ever spoke it or not, my belonging shaped my understanding that, if I worked hard enough, I could achieve anything.

For my friend who grew up in an immigrant family in Southern California, this sense of possibility looked different. She describes how belonging to her context shaped her sense of calling, both as a long-term sense of honor and obligation to her community and as her community's dream for her own professional opportunity. In both our cases, our most vivid sense of what it means to belong to God is interwoven with what it means to belong to others.

We are not blank slates waiting to hear from God. The places to which we belong set the foundation for what we believe is possible. Realities such as race, ethnicity, gender, physical location, church tradition, and really any other defining space deeply inform how we think about our calling, God, and what it looks like to listen to God about our calling.

Our belonging shapes our deeply held beliefs about the world and who we are in relation to the world.

2. Second doll: we have inherited a creative call.

If the innermost doll, our most central call, is to belong, the next doll we add is God's first call to humans: a creative calling. It is significant that our first story about God is one about God's creativity and work. Nestled within that story, we see evidence of God's first call to us, which is to be fruitful and multiply, to fill the earth and subdue it.

It's a call to create.

In Genesis 1, we come to know who God is through a picture of God as Maker. God creates the heavens and the earth and separates the night from day. God breathes life into existence by putting birds in the sky and fish in the sea. The cadence of God's creating is broken up only by God's delight in what is unfolding. The poet captures God's delight in creation with the phrase, "And God saw that it was good" (Gen. 1:10).

Creation is good.

Creating is good.

After we experience God as Creator, God makes humans. As part of the creation poem in Genesis 1, God says, "Let us make humans in our image, according to our likeness" (v. 26 NRSVUE). Yes, humans are made in the image of God, which is honestly kind of unbelievable. *We* are made to reflect the essence of the God who created us. We are made to work creatively in light of that essence.

God then blesses the first people and makes what is implicit explicit by commissioning them for their way forward: "Be fruitful and multiply and fill the earth and subdue it" (v. 28 NRSVUE). In the most literal sense, God's call to be fruitful means to have children, which is good, important, and creative work. But God's invitation to be fruitful goes far beyond bearing children. It extends to any sphere in which we find ourselves—friendships, activism, the office, church life, and so on. We are called to think and act as persons made in the image of a Maker. This is, of course, encouraging for those of us who see ourselves as creative or artistic. It's in our DNA! But it's also encouraging for those of us who don't always see ourselves in this way. This text sets an important foundation that, because we're made in the image of God, we *are* creative.

I suspect many of us need to recover this sense of creative calling. We need to lean in to the belief that we're called to be creative, especially when we're lost or looking for a way forward in the fog.

3. Third doll: we are called to participate in God's mission of redemption and restoration.

God's work is directional. God is working to redeem and restore. So, the next doll we can layer on is God's call to participate in that mission. Though patterns of redemption and restoration are found throughout Scripture, the language for how we want to frame this comes from 2 Corinthians 5. The text says this:

> All this is from God, who reconciled us to himself through Christ and has given us the ministry of reconciliation; that is, in Christ

God was reconciling the world to himself, not counting their trespasses against them, and entrusting the message of reconciliation to us. (vv. 18–19 NRSVUE)

Here, we get that God reconciled the world back to God through Jesus. With that, God has invited us into the ministry of reconciliation in the world. God's priorities of love, justice, healing, redemption, and wholeness are all part of that reconciling work. In all that we do, we are called to represent the redeeming, reconciling Christ in our lives.

Again, this calibration toward redemption can play out in both grand, mighty ways and ordinary, small ways. It can look like working to redeem big, broken systems that don't work for everyone or investing in ideal products that solve large problems. It can also be as simple as helping order a Google Drive folder that confuses and frustrates everyone on our team.

Think back to the three circles of control. Given your particular context and that which you have agency over, how is what you're doing already aligned with this aspect of God's calling? In ways big and small, God calls all of us to participate in the work of redemption and restoration. How are you actively following that call in the life you're living? How can it help give you guidance and direction, both now and when life changes?

4. Outermost doll: God does call us to particulars.

Once all our other nesting dolls are set, we can talk about God's call to particulars. See how long it took us to get to the particulars? While this is usually where most people start talking about calling, it's where Lisa and I think we should end. When we start here, we miss all that's nested within any sense of particulars. Yes, God calls each individual to particulars—particular people, places, moments, tasks, roles, and jobs. But these particulars flow from all our other callings. We show up as belongers, creatively working toward redemption and restoration in all aspects of our collective and individual lives.

Let's pause to note here that, while it is hopefully obvious that belonging to Jesus and creatively participating in God's work is for all Christians and not just religious leaders, the same is true for particular callings. Too often Lisa and I hear people say that they grew up in churches that prioritized the work of missionaries and pastors over that of businesspeople or parents. Remember, Paul says to the church in Corinth, "To the church of God that is in Corinth, to those sanctified in Christ Jesus and called to be his holy people, together with all those everywhere who call on the name of our Lord Jesus Christ—their Lord and ours" (1 Cor. 1:2).

Particular callings are for all, not for some.

Consider the story of Rahab. When Joshua is getting ready to lead the Israelites across the Jordan River into the promised land, he sends two spies to Jericho who are taken in by Rahab, a prostitute. She protects the spies and misdirects the king's men when they come searching for them. She begs the spies to show kindness to her family in return. And so, when Joshua and the Israelites take the city of Jericho, they spare the life of Rahab and her extended family.

Rahab professes her allegiance to the God of Israel and its people and puts herself at great risk. Why? In the Old Testament, we never really know. But when we open the book of Matthew, the first of the Gospels in the New Testament, we find a long genealogy of Jesus. This happens in several places in the Bible, and it's easy to breeze past those long lists of names. But right there, in verse 5, we see it: Rahab is the mother of Salmon and the grandmother to Boaz. Rahab, the prostitute who risks her own life and whose life is spared, is in the direct lineage of Jesus. Rahab, whose compass is set to God's calling.

Particular callings are just that: particular. Often, they're dynamic, not static. So, listening is key here. For most of us, God's particular callings don't come all at once, and they don't stay fixed for our entire lives. For example, do I feel a sense of calling to be a good grandmother? Not right now. My children are little. But might I someday? God willing. Did I feel called to attend a particular college? Yes. Is that calling a central part of what orients me today? No, it's not. These are particular callings for particular seasons.

Of course, some particular callings are more enduring, like my sense that God has called me to teach. In one way or another, I've known that about myself since I was a little girl, even before I had the language of calling.

Now, it's important to distinguish between calling and identity. Calling is both an invitation and a summons from God. Identity is our unique makeup. Though identity matters deeply for how we make sense of and respond to God's callings, identity and calling are not one and the same (a point we'll dive deeper into in the pages to come).

How should we think about all these different callings? The calls to belong, to create, to participate in redemption and restoration, to particulars. How do they relate to one another?

It's all meant to guide us and help us discern God's loving call. They're how we can set our compass. Together, they can work to point us toward our True North. They can move us forward in the right direction when we find ourselves navigating a life in flux.

Calibrate to God in the Fog

It's one thing to believe God calls us. It's another thing to be able to articulate a sense of calling, especially when we're in the fog. Then, more than ever, we have to calibrate to our sense of True North.

In essence, we're talking about *discernment*, which Ruth Haley Barton describes as "the capacity to recognize and respond to the presence and the activity of God—both in the ordinary moments and in the larger decisions of our lives."[8] If discernment lands in decision-making, calibration is about the space just before—the place where we put our hands in the water to sense which way the current is moving. The place where, like Roger, we cut the engine and quiet our minds so that we can hear the sounds of home and orient ourselves toward them.

Many theological traditions call what we're listening for the Holy Spirit. If that works for you, great. If not, you might think of it as *sensing God's loving presence in my life*. Whatever it looks or feels like to you, the need remains the same: to calibrate ourselves to God's calling in the midst of life's fog.

When life is in flux and disorientation sets in, we need to do the counterintuitive work of pausing and cutting the engine so that we can listen for the sounds that orient us. We need to return to our compass. But if we've never done the work to know what belonging to God feels and sounds like on shore—if we've never really excavated our own lives or deeply embraced God's calling to belong to God and others—we won't be able to attune to God's voice out at sea in the midst of the fog. So, we need to set and reset our compass to True North: God's ever-present, unconditional love.

> **COMMON POSTURE:** My navigational guidance system is based on external requirements and the expectations of others.
>
> **UNCOMMON POSTURE:** My navigational guidance system is a compass set to True North—God's love.

As Sean made his way in the fog of disruption in his job, he didn't quite know who he was apart from the expectations of others. He had no clear sense of God's calling, either to the particulars or to all that was nested within them. Honestly, the fog took a long time to begin to clear. But as it did, Sean emerged having developed the skills to withstand the ambiguity of the unfiguroutable and listen deeply for God's guidance on the way forward. Skills that would serve him well as he made a career pivot and was charged with a start-up venture outside of the academy.

Even though the rupture catalyzed so much pain, Sean would later describe it as a gift. Up until that point, he had been defined only by the old voices—the ones that had told him who they thought he should be. But now, without their influence, Sean was forced to both find a new job in order to make a living and, on a deeper level, discover more about who he was and what he wanted going forward. As he did, things became clearer.

In his own words, that calibrating to God's calling as his True North felt like an invitation: *Follow me into the dark, and I will be your light.*

A Prayer for Setting My Compass

Lord, I'm adrift in the fog.
I don't know exactly where I am or where I am headed.
But I trust that if I set my compass to you, the Truest North,
you will call me toward home.

I am grateful for your callings—
to belong,
to participate,
and to create
in particular ways.

To you I promise faithfulness.
I trust you are guiding my steps
even when I can't tell where we're going.

You promised your love and guidance,
even and especially when things feel foggy.
I know you will be with me.

I confess that being called by you is not about my comfort
    or safety
but rather about you.

I release my desire to know each step,
my fears, and my anxiety.
I trumpet your name as the one who always gets me
from here to there.

I set my compass to you,
for you are with me!
And for that I say

Amen.

7

Come Home
to Yourself

Thomas Merton writes, "There is only one problem on which all my existence, my peace, and my happiness depend: to discover myself in discovering God. If I find him I will find myself and if I find my true self I will find him."[1] Merton's reflection points to two deeply important parts of making our way through the fog: knowing God and knowing ourselves. The two are inextricably linked. We cannot know God in the deepest sense without knowing ourselves. And we cannot know ourselves in the deepest sense without knowing God.

In a world that's in flux, there is a whole lot of "We've never been here before!" and "Who in the world actually knows?" This near-constant undercurrent of ambiguous loss makes Pauline Boss's guideline that we have to be able to *re-create a sense of identity* feel all the more pressing. When everything can change so rapidly, we need to construct and reconstruct identity at every turn. The more we know about our core—the more we know ourselves—the more natural it will be for us to adapt.

After many years as a successful IT professional, Kevin perceived that the industry was heading into a period of rapid change. The future would need a new kind of IT consultant because technology was accelerating so quickly. Small and medium businesses would require a completely different set of tools than the ones current IT companies were offering. Because he saw the need and had developed true expertise to meet it, his friends and family encouraged him to make the jump from being an IT professional at a company to an IT consultant who would work with these businesses.

"Start your own business," they said.

"Pave the way toward the future," they said.

Two years into that process, Kevin ran into a big problem. None of his clients liked working with him. Sure, he had all the technical expertise one could want, but he was also arrogant and lacked the kind of emotional intelligence needed for client relationships. He couldn't stand it when someone didn't take his recommendations. He was used to being a decision-maker and an implementer.

Things felt too out of control for Kevin. He did not know how to serve clients well if they would not follow his direction. His business was falling apart, and his reputation was taking a hit. The crisis at work seeped into his home life in painful ways. He struggled to be present with his children, and his marriage was strained. They had taken a big risk, but now, Kevin doubted all that he was doing. Had he missed God's calling?

Kevin was completely bewildered about what to do next. All he knew was that a very real part of him was waking up to the fact that what got him to this point in his life wasn't going to get him where he wanted to go next. He didn't have where he wanted to go all figured out, but he did know that he wanted to save his marriage, be a present father, and be the kind of professional colleagues and clients valued. And, most importantly, he wanted to be faithful to God in the midst of it all.

While Kevin would end up on a yearslong journey of personal and professional transformation, first would come an intense nine months of self-discovery, in which he asked himself three big, new questions.

- *Who am I?*
- *Who am I not?*
- *What is mine to do?*

COMMON POSTURE: What should I do?

UNCOMMON POSTURE: Who am I? Who am I not?

The Work of Excavation

With these three questions, Kevin was on the verge of discovering a new Navigational Skill.

NAVIGATIONAL SKILL #6:

Come Home to Yourself

*I do the deep excavation work
needed to get to my true self.*

The work of excavating our truest selves is very hard and very slow. It happens little by little as we walk through many different seasons of flux. This is, according to Suzanne Stabile, "solitary work that cannot be done alone."[2] It feels kind of like assembling a giant jigsaw puzzle that we have to keep coming back to with fresh eyes. If we're fortunate, the people who, as Reyes says, have "loved us into being"[3] give us the corner pieces or maybe the edges. We know that, even then, the pieces won't always fit. We've got to trade them out, especially if there are wounds in those spaces. And the middle of the puzzle? This is the part that gives coherence to the picture; it's the part that takes a lifetime to put together.

We've already named that God's most central call for us is to *belong*—to God, to one another, and, yes, to ourselves. God's call to belong is predicated purely on the fact that we are God's beloved. This is good news that speaks to the deepest longings of our hearts. But here's the thing: though we belong to God from the very first day and nothing can take that from us, we will only know the fullest sense of belonging when we can embrace our truest sense of self. When we excavate our identity and calibrate it to our sense of belonging—our sense of home.

Most of us tote a whole lot of baggage with us as we make our way home. A lot of it is unconscious. This is why the process is waking up on the one hand and letting go on the other. In order to do this sort of self-excavation in the midst of flux, we have to be able both to attune to God's voice in the fog and to access our own emotions—especially those that are commonly deemed negative. By attending to these things first, we can eventually start to dig up what's underneath.

Our collective tendency is to minimize so-called negative emotions. We tell ourselves not to cry. We tell each other to look on the bright side. We reframe the toughest stuff as having silver linings. Instead of dealing with our sadness, fear, shame, or grief, we manage these emotions by developing, as Miriam Greenspan says, other attachments or ways of coping, like endurance and emotional control. These include:

muscling through
denying and avoiding by separating from our feelings

transcending or bypassing by ignoring and seeking some
   higher spiritual ground without actually going through
   the suffering
avenging—getting mad and getting even
escaping[4]

This last one is perhaps the most common way we avoid suffering in Western culture. We escape by bingeing our favorite shows, shopping excessively, or using addictive substances that alter our consciousness. We drink too much or scroll on our phones. We fill our lives with more and more activities. We do whatever we can to not sit with that which is hard to feel.[5]

Excavation requires us to dig deeper. That means we have to have the space to go deep. To move beyond the negative feelings and the ways in which we cope with or manage them. To tune our ears to God's voice and align our compass to God's leading. To do the work to find our true identity—our true self—underneath.

Who Am I? Who Am I Not?

So, how do we come home to our truest selves? Lisa and I think it starts by asking ourselves Kevin's first two big questions:

- *Who am I?*
- *Who am I not?*

The first has been asked in a multitude of ways by philosophers and theologians across the ages. It is both an existential question and a personal one—simultaneously lofty and practical.

- *What is the meaning of life more broadly?*
- *What is the meaning of my life specifically?*

- *What are humans here to do?*
- *Who am I uniquely created to be?*
- *How do I offer who I am to the world?*

Too often, we are defined by external forces—the systems we are a part of and the circumstances we find ourselves in.

We are in customer service. We are divorced. We are drowning in responsibilities. We are a parent. The list goes on.

To find our way forward in the fog, we have to find our true self—who we are deep down inside—regardless of the circumstances we find ourselves in.

> **COMMON POSTURE:** I am defined by my performance and productivity, by external forces and circumstances.
>
> **UNCOMMON POSTURE:** I am defined by my identity in Christ and my belonging. I am loved and worthy because of who God made me to be.

In his landmark book on leadership, *A Failure of Nerve*, Edwin Friedman leverages Murray Bowen's family systems work and applies it to leadership and healthy organizational systems. Friedman says that the well-defined leader is one who does not emotionally enmesh in the systems they are part of. In other words, they don't contribute to, cause drama in, or get caught up in reactivity cycles. However, they also don't detach or cut and run when things get challenging. Instead, they stay present to others in a healthy, nonattached, non-anxious way.[6] The leaders who can do this know who they are and who they are not. Because they have defined themselves in a way that's not dependent on the system, the threat of uncertainty doesn't send them into reactivity. Their non-anxious presence turns down the heat, both for themselves and for others, in the midst of confusion.

Even if we're not leading an organization, we want to engage with change in the same way. We are not defined by it. We do not engage with it reactively. We step back and ask important and healthy questions. All this requires us to have a strong sense of self-identity that's not dependent on external factors.

Kevin was the opposite of non-anxious. He was caught in reaction loops in a way that revealed how much his sense of identity hinged on his new IT business. If a client didn't like his ideas, that would send him into a tailspin and make him grouchy all day long. If someone didn't respond to his email promptly, he would spend his evening checking his phone instead of being present with his kids. He didn't know who he was without that job, and his reactions showed it.

Eventually, Kevin hired Lisa (yes, our Lisa!) as his leadership coach. Lisa's first order of business was to help him take an emotional step back from the situation he was in so that he could press into the work of differentiating himself from his career. So that he could ask the tough questions that would help him peel away the layers of all his reactivity and get down to who he really was.

The work of growing into ourselves, guided by the grace of God, is core to the path of navigating flux. And yet many of us naturally resist this work. Maybe it's because we are beholden to that which feels urgent—the big presentation, the laundry, the looming decision. Or we've been taught that investing in ourselves is selfish or somehow in contrast to what God might want for us.

Here's the thing: when we don't know ourselves deeply, our choices are too easily driven by factors outside of ourselves. What we do can become driven by guilt, fear, or misplaced obligation to others. We end up working beyond our means to please everyone or taking shortcuts because we're overwhelmed. We may even end up like Kevin, who felt most secure when he was the expert in the room. Either way, we find our sense of home in a limited part of ourselves. That's like spending our whole lives in a single room of our house! When we white-knuckle the limited stories we've told ourselves for so long, that baggage blocks us from connecting with a deeper sense of our identity. It keeps us from knowing who we are and who we aren't. And when we don't know that, we can't possibly show up as our full selves or have a great sense of what is ours to do and what isn't.[7]

Loving Ourselves

One of the most familiar stories in the Christian tradition is that of the Good Samaritan. It starts with a lawyer questioning Jesus about eternal life. Jesus, turning it back on the lawyer, asks him what is written in the law about how to live. The lawyer replies, "'Love the Lord your God with all your heart and with all your soul and with all your strength and with all your mind'; and, 'Love your neighbor as yourself'" (Luke 10:27).

Then Jesus goes on to tell the story of the Good Samaritan as an example of what it looks like to be a good neighbor. A man, having been robbed and beaten, is lying by the side of the road, unable to get up. Two different men notice him, but instead of going to help him, they move away, taking extra effort to keep their distance. A third man, a Samaritan, notices the one in need and goes toward him, using his own resources to help the man and very likely risking his own safety for the sake of helping the one who is hurt.

Over the past decade, the story of the Good Samaritan has radically reoriented my life. I have learned to see myself in each of the characters in the story—the seemingly rushed elites who turn away from pain, the one whose compassion motivates them to reorient their time and resources in response to others, and the wounded traveler who cannot move forward without the help of another. I've sensed God's own invitation to me through this passage is to honor all of these parts of me, even if I would rather the shameful, rushed me and the desperate, pained me never took center stage.

The point is this: in order to love our neighbors with compassion, we must first love ourselves with compassion—the good, bad, and ugly. And in order to get to know and love all of ourselves with compassion, we must believe that God first loves us. We can take a cue from Merton's quote that opened this chapter. If we find and love God, we will find ourselves. If we find and love our truest selves, we will find God.

The journey of discovering ourselves and thus the journey of discerning our calling is a lifelong undertaking. (Remember: identity and calling are distinct but interdependent.) The earlier we begin to undertake this journey, the healthier our relationships will be with God and others. That health will inevitably strengthen our ability to participate in God's work in the world via our work, families, communities, and more. The more we focus on loving ourselves in seasons of flux, the more we'll be able to move through the fog with our identity firmly intact.

When we learn to love ourselves—even the toughest parts of us—we grow in our capacity to know ourselves more deeply and show up more honestly wherever we are. When Paul writes to the church in Rome, he encourages them to offer every part of their lives to God. Eugene Peterson's modern rewording of this passage reads, "Take your everyday, ordinary life—your sleeping, eating, going-to-work, and walking around life—and place it before God as an offering" (Rom. 12:1 MSG).

By offering our lives to God, we are embracing God's grace and love in our lives. And when we do, the next verse says we will "be changed from the inside out." Importantly, this change happens as a result of God's loving *grace*, not our own effort. Our job is to show up to the work, but "God brings the best out of you, develops well-formed maturity in you" (v. 2 MSG).

If you've ever been around someone who knows themselves well and has the kind of humble confidence in God's love described here, then you know just how much of a gift this type of person is. They are not perfect. Someone who really knows God's love is willing to admit their own mistakes because they trust that God is merciful. Paul himself says that "Christ Jesus came into the world to save sinners—of whom I am the worst" (1 Tim. 1:15). Inevitably, this makes them a joy to be around in so many ways because they know themselves and love themselves, wholly and honestly. Because of this well-formed identity, they don't make it all about themselves; in fact, they seem to forget themselves entirely.[8]

As we engage in the work of excavating who we are, we can know that, as Paul says, "The only accurate way to understand ourselves is by what God is and by what he does for us, not by what we are and what we do for him" (Rom. 12:3 MSG). We can slowly release any need to build our identity on something other than God as we embrace all that God has lovingly done for us. As we do this, our fragile ego—the false self—is replaced with our rootedness in our identity in Christ.[9] This is slow work, one puzzle piece at a time.

Other Bible translations talk about this way of perceiving ourselves as *sober judgment*—the ability to see ourselves in relation to God and others with clarity and humility. Again, I don't mean self-deprecation but rather an honest understanding of who we are and who we aren't.

One of the ways we can know we're growing toward this is when we can genuinely receive criticism—even judgment—from others as an opportunity to learn and grow. When life is in flux and circumstances are changing, there's often stuff that's hard to hear. Sometimes people give feedback with grace, and other times it hits harder. But even when someone says something hurtful or out of line, our ability to trust God's love is connected to our desire to know ourselves deeply enough to sort through what's said and take any kernel of truth to heart. We each have been given good gifts to tend and cultivate, but we can't really grow in who we are if we don't hear this kind of feedback.

Excavating Who We Are

When we enter the fog, chances are we will want to learn new things about ourselves. Each of us has much to offer in the midst of flux, but not everything is ours to do. The verses that come next in Paul's letter to the Romans describe the gifts needed for the people of God to serve the world. These gifts are distributed to all of us uniquely, and we need each other to completely give our lives and work back to God together.

In order to understand how we might contribute to the whole, we have to look even more closely at our own unique blueprint. We have to come to know our own true giftings.

COMMON POSTURE: I can play many roles, whatever is needed to get the job done.

UNCOMMON POSTURE: What is mine to do? There are only a few roles I am uniquely created to inhabit, and when I take on too much and overextend, everyone loses.

That brings us to the third question Kevin had to ask himself:

- *What is mine to do?*

It's a uniquely modern question to ask—with the assumption that the world is our oyster. It signals a kind of privilege that most people in human history simply haven't had or don't have. Ironically, asking this question with a blank slate, or in an attempt to find our passion—in hopes that it will guide us toward what we ought to do—is not usually helpful or realistic. A quest to find our one true passion, rooted in endless possibilities, is overwhelming and not all that pragmatic.

While it's a freeing thing to realize that not everything is ours to do, it's also a difficult one. Getting clear is long, slow work that happens when we look back and listen to our own lives and ask what they are teaching us. More puzzle pieces.

Our circumstances rarely provide space to reflect on what is uniquely ours to do. Just as we are collectively called to belong to God and one another, we are each made in particular and distinct ways. Deeply knowing ourselves—both what is true about us as humans made in God's image and what is uniquely true about us as individuals—is part of how we know which direction to move when the fog sets in.

> If you're a people person, chances are you're going to move forward via relationships.
>
> If you like to have the facts spelled out, you might navigate flux by charting some spreadsheets.
>
> If you're a musician, you might need to feel your way forward by getting out your guitar.

To figure out our own way forward in the fog, we need to do the work of excavating who we are. While there are many good frameworks and tools for doing this kind of work, for our purposes here we'll focus just on two.

1. Understand our stance toward time and how it impacts our perception of change.

Some people hate personality tests. Lisa and I are not those people. I, for one, have taken each one four times just for fun.

Because the work of navigating disruption requires us to wrestle with our inner selves, Lisa and I find particular value in the Enneagram.[10] The Enneagram is an ancient wisdom personality system that helps us gain insight into various aspects of who we are and how we move in the world. I am an Enneagram Seven, commonly dubbed the Enthusiast. Lisa is an Enneagram Eight, known as the Challenger. She's also an Enneagram expert. Beyond the nine types, there are different groupings within the tool itself that can be helpful in this work of coming home to our true selves. One of these has to do with our natural *orientation to time*, which has implications for how we feel about and handle change. Even if you don't know your type (or hate the Enneagram) you might identify with a particular orientation toward time.

Each of us has a primary way in which we orient in relation to time that impacts how we perceive and deal with change. If you know your type, the following will be helpful to your excavation work. If you don't, that's okay too! Read on to see where you might find yourself.

Orientation to the future (types Three, Seven, and Eight). If our natural orientation toward time is the future, we are prone to focus on *what's next*. It can be easy to ignore the past, and we can have a hard time staying present in the present. In fact, looking toward the future can be a way to repress our current emotions and ignore that which we'd rather not see about ourselves and others. At first glance, it can seem like those of us oriented toward the future like or are at least amenable to change. We can envision it, wrap our brains around it, and therefore move toward it. But when we look closer, the future-oriented actually have a more complicated relationship to change. We want to get out ahead of it—to either control it, plan for it, fantasize about it, or ensure we're not controlled by it in any way.

Those of us oriented toward the future will need to learn to stop and reflect on the past. To ask questions while we're in the midst of flux about what worked, what didn't, and what we might learn from those experiences. The big challenge for us is to be present in the here and now and not dismiss what can be learned from the past as we make our way forward in the fog.

If you sense that you are oriented toward the future, the path toward growth for the sake of navigating change is through pause and reflection. Think back to the way Roger got home safely. What did he do? He paused, cut the engine, listened, and then moved incrementally forward without trying to force or control either the ocean or the fog. He got home by stopping long enough to listen for the signs of it. To trust himself to guide his way toward the future.

Orientation to the past (types Four, Five, and Nine). If our natural stance toward time is the past, we tend to focus on what has already happened. That means that, in flux, we use the past as a reference point for framing both the present and the future. When those of us who are oriented toward the past think about the past, we feel it deeply and wonder how it will inform the change we're experiencing now. Our fears about what might happen can cause us to withdraw to our inner worlds and feel so stuck that we just keep slowing down.

Roger and his friends eventually had to make decisions about which way to go. Even if they risked getting it wrong, they had to move. In the midst of fog, the path toward growth for past-oriented types is to do the same: to consciously and intentionally engage in what is happening right in front of us. To listen to the waves. To smell the salty air. To feel our own fear so that we are alerted to our need to move toward others as a way to move beyond being emotionally stuck and grow more receptive to change. Plus, we can look back and remember all the times when things worked out or when we learned as a result of failure. Then we can better trust that whatever happens will not undo us. As we move toward others, we can start to look toward the future with hope and possibility, knowing that we will be okay even if we have to go deeper into the fog.

Orientation to the present (types One, Two, and Six). If our natural stance toward time is present, then we are focused on what is right in front of us. We make sense of what's happening in the present in relation to what's happening with others, and this will inform how we think and feel about change. If we are present-oriented, we might worry about the future or want to get change *absolutely right* in order to avoid potential fallout later on. We typically go hard and feel big, but we can often repress our thinking. We do think, but more in the reactive, go fast, make it all happen sense. Here, we can get stuck in unproductive reaction loops or internal monologues.

Considering the future and intentionally moving toward it—despite the risk of getting it wrong, failing, or being deemed unhelpful—can help us get unstuck. The goal is to move forward incrementally and iteratively toward the future by building in mechanisms for reflection along the way. While being sober about reality, Roger and his friends had to hold hope that they would indeed get home. They had to imagine themselves standing on the dock just as they had many times before. Letting ourselves look out to the horizon, not only to focus on the stuff we fear but to give ample space for what we hope for, is the path toward growth for those of us oriented toward the present.

2. Collect and listen to the pieces of our lives.

As we consider who we are and how we navigate life in flux, we have to regularly and intentionally remember what makes us who we are. We are shaped and formed by both the genetic code placed in each one of us and the world around us. We spend our lifetime putting the puzzle together—looking into our own stories to find the patterns that reveal who we are and how we move when we are offering our best to the world. These stories also have a shadow side that shows us where we can over-function and get in our own way, as well as where we might unintentionally step on others. As we put the pieces of our own lives together, it's important to see it all through the lens of love. Remember, God's love and the love of others set the foundation from which we can do this work.

Our stories over the arc of our lifetime help us see and learn what it looks like to bring our best (and yes, sometimes our worst) to ourselves and to others. Our stories can help us notice where we try to flee the present, forget the past, or fight the future. As we uncover new insights into how we move through the world, we'll find patterns and habits that we can choose to change. We can let go of the things that are keeping us stuck in unhealthy patterns, relationships, and circumstances. We can identify trauma and pain that, in the context of a professional therapeutic relationship, can be worked with and worked through toward healing. As we wake up and let go, we know we do not always have the ability or agency to change our external environment, but we can always change how we choose to respond.

A way to remember our own stories for the sake of navigating change is to remember times when we brought the very best of who we were to an endeavor.[11] Over the arc of a lifetime, when we begin to understand ourselves at our best, we gain an increasingly clearer picture of who we are (and who we are not) when we are living into who God made us to be. Researchers often call this *intrinsic motivation*.[12]

One method to dig deep into motivational energy is in an interview format. Lisa and I have both used this strategy in cohorts we've developed. In the cohort program Lisa ran for many years, she divided the participants into groups of three—a listener/notetaker, an interviewer, and an interviewee. The goal was to have each interviewee remember a time they did something well, enjoyed doing it, and achieved a deeply satisfying result.[13]

The structure of such interviews goes like this:

- What did you do? (Ask for a brief description of the achievement.)
- How did you go about doing it? (Listen for the actions— the verbs. Ask probing questions, using those verbs as doors; do not ask *why* questions.)
- What was most satisfying for you? (Ask this a couple of times, perhaps in slightly different ways.)

In just two or three interviews, the patterns emerge quickly. The nature of the interview itself requires both the listener and the interviewer to really attend to the person telling their story. The interviewee experiences being truly listened to in a way they may never have before. Often strong emotions surface as people recover pieces of themselves they have long suppressed in service of building skills and competence. Knowing these pieces of ourselves helps us to increasingly make better choices (often hard ones!) about what we say yes to and what we say no to. This is a critical component to responding to God's calling, as it helps us understand where we belong and how we can best contribute.

We most often think of achievements through the lens of accolades or awards—some sort of external recognition. These feel good for a bit, but their shine can eventually wear off. If an accomplishment does not intrinsically motivate us, it will not sustain our energy or interest over time. In contrast, remembering something we did well, we enjoyed, and that gave us deep satisfaction evokes a quite different response. These are often not things for which we have received recognition but rather smaller doings in which we experienced a deep kind of personal satisfaction.

When I first participated in an interview like this, I remember recalling the leaf collection business I started when I was ten and helping a star player get her swing back as a softball coach. Getting my PhD was not on the list. Birthing my kids was also absent. Helping my daughter grow as a reader? That was there! As I started to collect the pieces of my own life, even before an expert analyzed my results, I realized that I love helping people, individuals and groups, achieve their potential. That is deeply intrinsically motivating for me. So, no matter what I sense God calling me to do, I know that if it involves people moving toward their own potential, focusing on the task this way will be sustaining for me.

Knowing this also helps me reframe things, especially in flux. For example, if I'm frustrated that my kids won't go to bed, I might reframe our bedtime struggles as an opportunity to help my kids develop lifelong sleep habits. Or if I'm unsure how to deal with a difficult personnel issue, I can reframe it as an opportunity to help all involved move toward their potential. Knowing myself more intimately helps me make shifts like these.

Recovering the Broken Pieces

Lisa and I have said several times that doing this work is like a puzzle, and that's true. But what about when things feel messy? When the pieces feel broken? When they just don't seem to fit? The ancient Japanese art of *kintsugi* is instructive for how we might process the stories of our lives with all their goodness and brokenness. Kintsugi literally means "to mend or repair with gold."[14] The process is most often done with pieces of pottery that have been broken. In the aftermath of the Japanese earthquake and tsunami of 2011 near the city of Sendai, artist Kunio Nakomura's small studio exploded with people who wanted to repair their familiar bowls and cups as a way to experience healing and retain a piece of home in the midst of so much loss.[15]

In other words, they wanted to put their broken pieces back together in a new, beautiful way.

Makoto Fujimura, an artist and cultural catalyst who practices kintsugi, suggests that this art form can be transferred to other elements that need to be mended and restored. He reflects, "The gold poured into the fissures is much like the Spirit flowing into our lives and is fundamentally connected to our trauma and healing."[16]

When parts of our stories feel broken or fragmented, the path to navigating the fog might be to know ourselves more deeply by putting the pieces together with metaphorical gold, trusting that God is present and vibrant in the mending.

Remember our friend Kevin, struggling in his new IT business? Naturally oriented toward the present, he had to slowly reflect on both the pain and success of the past. He had unresolved pain from childhood that had tremendous implications for how he entered relationships. It's no wonder he led with technical competence and his relational walls up.

As he slowly started shifting away from a performative mindset and toward one of trying to understand who he was in God and in the context of others, Kevin felt himself start to move from *I am what I do and what I earn* to the new mindset *I am a child of God, and I am loved, no matter what.* His fissures didn't mend quickly; some of them not at all. But love was seeping into the broken cracks and crevices to rejoin the broken pieces.

Eventually, Kevin started to feel like his new business might not be fully aligned with who he actually was and how he was wired. He grew more comfortable with imagining the future as one in which God would always be with him, calling him to belong and participate in *repair* wherever he was. As he started to let go of some of the vision he was white-knuckling, he had new space to test the waters on some new projects that reflected where he had been successful and satisfied in the past.

And this time, he did it with a greater sense of who he was—and, therefore, of who God was—under his feet.

In kintsugi, an artist's work of repair can take a year or more. Yes, there are shortcuts that enable a bowl or mug to be more quickly repaired.[17] But if the artist has not followed a careful process over time, the repair may not hold up. The same is true for us. We may want to take shortcuts and quick fixes in our journey, but doing so will not lead us to repair. It won't mend us as we make our way forward in the fog.

Sorting out the pieces of our own lives, however, will. Then, we can rest securely in the love of the One who made us—the One who will guide us home.

A Prayer for When
I'm Learning about Myself

Lord, I long to know you,
and I am learning that I cannot truly know you until I
know myself.

As I look at the parts of myself, help me to accept what I see.
To acknowledge my protective shell,
to name what feels broken,
and to release the habits that keep me feeling safe but
also keep me stuck.

Sometimes I can't help but hide behind a mask of my
own creation.

Help me peel back the layers of performance and productivity,
releasing the expectations of others
and accepting what is mine to do.

In this fog, help me to more deeply understand
who you have made me to be
and to love myself,
just as you love me.

Amen.

Don't Go It Alone

When I was ten years old, my grandparents moved in across the street from us. We knew that my grandpa had Alzheimer's and that my grandma needed more support in his care. It was the early nineties, so we didn't know as much about Alzheimer's then as we do today. We had no idea how moving him out of his home would accelerate his dementia. Soon after they moved in, he moved back out—this time to a nursing home where he could get more care.

Left behind on a quiet street, living in two houses that looked at each other, were my mom, my grandma, and me. My mom would often send me across the street, saying something like, "Go help your grandma." My grandma was a woman of the garden, but it had become harder for her to get down on her knees, and her hands didn't always cooperate. Not then nor ever have I had a green thumb. I have whatever the opposite of a green thumb is. But, on more than one occasion when my mom sent me over, Grandma would meet me at the door with a job in the garden. See, she'd been sitting inside all day, frustrated by the fact that she couldn't just go out and do what she wanted to in the garden. On those days, I became quite literally her hands.

"What do you want me to do today, Grandma?"

"Move that rosebush, Michaela."

"Ok, Grandma. Where would you like it?"

"Six inches to the right."

I kid you not: I spent a portion of my early teenage years learning to move bushes six inches to the right.

Almost always, when I was taking on one of these projects, she would poke her head out the back door and call for me to come inside when I was done. There I trusted I would find a plate of warm cookies and a chair at Grandma's table. As we sat and talked about whatever it was we talked about, I felt safe, seen, and loved. I learned about her early career ambitions—how good she was at math. I learned about her boyfriends, especially Eddie. I learned about how she and her sisters would dance the night away as teenagers to escape the hardship of Depression-era life on the prairie.

What I couldn't see then that I'm wondering now is the motivation for this work. Maybe Grandma wasn't just fussing over plants. Maybe she was coming up with jobs for me in the garden that would usher me toward her table. With my grandpa moved out of her house and me on the edge of my teenage years, we were both living in the in-between. There was a lot to grieve and a lot to wonder. But there at her table, I knew I was safe and seen. I knew I was home.

COMMON POSTURE: I don't need help from anyone.

UNCOMMON POSTURE: I benefit from trusted relationships of mutuality, even when it is hard and uncomfortable.

These chores in the garden and especially our conversations afterward shaped my imagination of what a good life looks like. Of course, we can't shield ourselves from pain or circumvent the grief that comes crashing in as life changes. But even when life is at its worst, if we have someone safe to sit down and eat cookies with, love can still have the final word.

NAVIGATIONAL SKILL #7:

Don't Go It Alone

I build core relationships of trust and vulnerability to provide myself with safety and support when I am navigating hard things.

A Loneliness Epidemic

The reality is so many of us feel alone. The US Surgeon General's office describes loneliness this way:

> A subjective distressing experience that results from perceived isolation or inadequate meaningful connections, where inadequate refers to the discrepancy or unmet need between an individual's preferred and actual experience.[1]

A lack of meaningful connections. Perceived isolation. Unmet needs between our hopes and expectations. Not good, right?

Well, the statistics are sobering at best and frightening at worst. Experts report that more than three in five Americans are lonely.[2] The stats only get bleaker as we focus in on specifics. Loneliness is highest among Gen Z.[3] A third of people age forty-five and up feel lonely. One-fourth of people age sixty-five and up are socially isolated.[4] Across the generations, people feel lonely, isolated, and without the kind of warm, loving relationships humans need. As the world feels more uncertain—as we try to navigate our way through the fog of change and disruption— this trend toward loneliness becomes even more concerning.

Vivek H. Murthy, the nineteenth and twenty-first US surgeon general, put out an official advisory about the effects of loneliness in 2023, writing:

> Loneliness is far more than just a bad feeling—it harms both individual and societal health. It is associated with greater risk of cardiovascular diseases, dementia, stroke, depression, anxiety, and premature death. The mortality impact of being socially disconnected is similar to that caused by smoking up to 15 cigarettes a day.[5]

Sound the alarm.

Our disconnection from each other—perceived and actual—is literally killing us. We desperately need to recover what it looks like to not go it alone.

One of the most fascinating studies on what humans need to live a meaningful, satisfied life started in 1938 and continues today. The Harvard Study of Adult Development has followed the lives of two generations of adults, monitoring everything from physical health levels to alcohol usage to mental well-being. Their data is sophisticated, nuanced, and as close to comprehensive as we have—at least for the participants who are in the study.

At the heart of the research findings is one clear fact: people need each other.[6] We're hardwired for connection, and anything that threatens it comes at a detriment to our health. In a recent book chronicling the study, its current research directors write, "To say that human beings require warm relationships is no touchy-feely idea. It is a hard fact. Scientific studies have told us again and again: human beings need nutrition, we need exercise, we need purpose, and we need each other."[7]

We need purpose, and *we need each other.*

Well, just because we need something doesn't mean we're getting it. We've sacrificed so much on the altar of Western individualism. Murthy's report is clear: loneliness is not an individual problem. There are cultural, communal, and societal dynamics that drive both connection and disconnection. Solving our loneliness epidemic is not nearly as simple as getting more friends.

In an interview for the *New York Times* with Tish Harrison Warren, psychiatrist and author Curt Thompson makes a link between the burnout that has run rampant the last few years in American culture and our epidemic of loneliness. He argues that because the Western imagination is a product of modernity, it's no wonder we have built our lives around "any number of practices . . . that have us moving further and further away from each other."[8] We are less known by our neighbors. We make little room for spontaneity in our schedules. We've lost the art of lingering.

We've lost our ability to find one another in the fog.

We all likely know that there are compelling links between feelings of loneliness and greater technology usage, particularly social media.[9] Ironic as it is, the thing designed to connect us is the thing that makes us feel more alone than ever. Many are sounding the siren for an intentional return to not only the physical world but the actual real-life presence of others.

When we feel alone, we can't access what it takes to sustain the way forward. We don't have the meaningful relationships that make life feel not only possible but worth it.

Said another way, if we are all alone out at sea, it is much harder to get home.

The Right Relationships

When we're lonely, we are disconnected from what God intends for us. We are left alone with a self who is hard to know because part of how we come to know ourselves is through others. It's through the building of mutually beneficial relationships.

Take Liz, for example. She couldn't ignore the nagging feeling in her gut that she had to break off her engagement. She loved Henry, but their relationship just wasn't good. Liz had come from a family with really tough dynamics, and she saw those dynamics starting to play out with her soon-to-be husband. So, she ran. Leaving was the right choice, but it left her with lingering doubt about whether she could trust her own decision-making when it came to intimate relationships or even trusted friends.

After the breakup, Liz spent an intense season learning more about herself and the systems that had formed her. She invested in the slow work of positive, healthy connections. In all the reflection she did, she actually mapped her healthy relationships. The relationships where she didn't have to think about being herself or impressing anyone. The people with whom she felt truly comfortable, safe, and loved.

She had an aunt who loved her and supported her unconditionally but also told her the truth when she needed to hear it. She had a few college friends she still liked hanging out with, as well as some new friends from yoga and work. She also got a new therapist. For Liz, these were the relationships she needed to help her move forward when her life was in flux.

Murthy and his team describe three components of social connection that are ideally present in an individual's life: structure, function, and quality.

Structure refers to the number and variety of relationships one has. For Liz, she had her family, her work friends, her college friends, her yoga friends, and her therapist.

Function is the degree to which different relationships serve our relational needs. For example, Liz felt emotional support from her aunt, but not so much from her family or her work friends.

Quality includes the positive and negative aspects of relationships amid various interactions. Liz was not at all satisfied in her romantic relationship; that's why she broke it off. And she wasn't satisfied with her immediate family members either. The quality of her college relationships had gone down now that they were all coupled up while she was single. With that, she felt the pangs of being on the outside when they all did couples night without her now.[10]

We cannot navigate flux without each other. In this day and age, connection is not a given. In order to establish and maintain healthy relationships, we have to consider the quality of our relationships, how they function in our lives, and the very structure of how we relate and socialize with one another.

We have to figure out who will stand in the fog alongside us.

Designed for Relationship

On the first pages of the Bible, God is poetically depicted as saying, "Let us make humans in our image" (Gen. 1:26 NRSVUE). There's so much in these seven words.

Creation.

The *imago Dei*.

The Trinity.

Who in the world is *us*? It's honestly hard to know exactly what the ancient Israelites would have meant by this plurality. One commonly supported interpretation is to understand *us* through the lens of the Christian doctrine of the Trinity.

While nowhere in the Bible does it explicitly say that God is three in one, one in three, that's how we've come to interpret the relationship between God the Creator, Jesus Christ, and the Holy Spirit. Theologian Stanley Grenz writes:

> The first followers of Jesus inherited from their Old Testament background the strict allegiance to the one God—the God of Abraham, Isaac, and Jacob. But they had also come to confess Jesus as the risen and exalted Lord. In addition, they were conscious of

the ongoing divine presence within their community, a presence provided by the Holy Spirit.[11]

Since those early days, Christians have continued to experience God as multifaceted but ultimately one God.[12]

There's a lot we could say about the Trinity. For nearly two thousand years, theologians have worked to do just that. While Lisa and I won't pretend to add new ideas to the sensemaking, we do want to highlight a couple aspects of trinitarian theology that set the stage for how we might relate to one another.

1. God is relational.

2. God is love.

3. Love meets us in suffering.

In John 10, Jesus paints a picture of belonging to a relational, loving God who meets us in our suffering. He says, "The thief comes only to steal and kill and destroy; I have come that they may have life, and have it to the full. I am the good shepherd. The good shepherd lays down his life for the sheep" (vv. 10–11). Jesus the Good Shepherd knows us, sees us, and comes for us when we go astray. He calls us by name, and, as we come to know the voice of our Shepherd, we are safely at home in God's love. When heartache or danger comes for us, God's love is passionate enough that the Shepherd walks toward the danger, not away. That's why Jesus embodies, as theologian Jürgen Moltmann says, "the voluntary laying oneself open to another and allowing oneself to be intimately affected by him; that is to say, the suffering of passionate love."[13] Bonded by love, he is at once the Good Shepherd and the Suffering Christ.

Grenz writes, "But what is the bond that unites the Triune God we have come to know? The key to the answer to our query lies in the biblical declaration, 'God is love' (1 John 4:8, 16)."[14]

God is one.

God is three.

Creator, Redeemer, and Sustainer.

These are distinct yet unified, bonded together by a love that transcends all and can bear all.

Amazingly, the love of God is not reserved for the members of the Trinity. God's love makes its way to us in rather radical forms, including through the person of Jesus, who was sent by love to meet us in our suffering. The promise of God is this:

> The LORD himself goes before you and will be with you; he will never leave you nor forsake you. Do not be afraid; do not be discouraged. (Deut. 31:8)

In this, we receive not only the declaration that God is with us but the welcome to deeply belong to the divine. This invitation becomes the vehicle for both our communion with God and our relationships with others. In short, we were designed for relationship. We were designed for the thing we need most in a life in flux.

Dietrich Bonhoeffer wrote *Life Together*, a book on Christian discipleship, against the backdrop of Nazi Germany in 1938. It was a time when both people of the Jewish faith and those who supported the faithful were being persecuted. Grounded honestly in the tragedy that was happening around him, Bonhoeffer makes the case that community is both a hard and a necessary element for wholeness in a disorienting world:

> The physical presence of other Christians is a source of incomparable joy and strength to the believer. . . . It is easily forgotten that the fellowship of Christian brethren is a gift of grace, a gift of the Kingdom of God that any day may be taken from us.[15]

For Bonhoeffer, the gift of grace that was fellowship was ultimately taken away as he stood for justice in the face of a brutal and evil regime. Bonhoeffer lived in disorienting, uncertain, and terrifying times. And yet, if you study his life and teachings, you can see his deep and abiding relationships, first with Jesus and then with communities of people he was deeply committed to, are what helped him make the choices he did to respond to God's calling, even when it threatened and ultimately cost him his life.

God intends for us to come to know love together and through each other. Stanley Grenz goes as far as to say that "the image of God can only be expressed in human community."[16] That means when we isolate from other people, we also feel isolated from God. Because God's image is expressed in love, we express God's image to each other through love. And because God comes to us as the Good Shepherd and the Suffering Christ, our capacity to relate to others in suffering is part of how we bear the image of God to one another.

Liz's aunt and therapist. Bonhoeffer's friends and family. Those trusted relationships that bring each of us God's love.

It's from this sense of deep community that we come to understand who we really are. The work of excavating ourselves is intertwined with our coming home to others. Grenz writes, "Only by being persons in community do we find our true identity— that form of the world toward which our 'openness to the world,' our restless shaping and reshaping of our environment, is intended to point us."[17]

Point us toward True North.

Point us the way we need to go in the fog.

Point us home.

But modern life is hard. With each year that passes, it seems new challenges are around every corner. We're dealing with things that would have been simply unimaginable to generations before us. Of course, the rapid pace of change and increasingly connected society create both new obstacles and new opportunities. When things get really, really hard or complicated, as they so often do, basic human connection can get relegated to the sidelines. It is hard to reach out to others when we feel like we're lost in the fog. It's hard to do hard things. It is even harder to do them if we feel alone. We can instead opt for any number of coping mechanisms. And, in this, our sense of belonging is traded for isolation.

In other words, we lose our sense of home.

So, how do we combat this? By holding two truths at the same time: relationships can be awfully hard, *and* we desperately need them to navigate our way through life in flux.

> **COMMON POSTURE:** Relationships are hard and difficult. I don't have the time or energy to invest in them.
>
> **UNCOMMON POSTURE:** Relationships are hard and difficult, and they are worth investing in deeply, even when it gets challenging. Nothing is more important than trusted, positive relationships.

Expect the Unexpected

On the day after Christmas in 2004, just before breakfast in Indonesia, a 9.1 magnitude earthquake struck. Not only did the earthquake take a heartbreaking toll in the provinces of Aceh and North Sumatra but it also triggered what experts describe as the deadliest tsunami in known history. In the wake of the devastation, images of desperation—people searching for their mothers and brothers and friends—were plastered all over the news. Tragically, between the earthquake and the subsequent tsunami, it is estimated that nearly 250,000 lives were lost.[18] So many of those searching never found who they were looking for.

As part of the relief effort, teams of mental health professionals were sent over from the United States to provide trauma and grief counseling. Shortly after the initial response was underway, a team of researchers led by Elizabeth Frankenberg, Cecep Sumantri, and Duncan Thomas designed and launched a longitudinal research project that came to be known as the Study of the Tsunami Aftermath and Recovery (STAR).[19] What they observed is noteworthy. Of course, people ached with grief, especially in the early months. But over time, the study revealed some interesting findings.

> Among all the results, one characteristic stands out. "The most startling thing we've seen is the level of resilience the population has shown," Frankenberg said. Thomas added, "There was a huge amount of psychosocial stress, and what's astonishing is a lot of the people who had high levels of post-traumatic stress reactivity were able to rebuild their lives, broadly speaking, in ways that really surprised me."[20]

On the whole, when the researchers went back ten years later, they found much lower rates of post-traumatic stress disorder, anxiety, and depression than they had predicted. This was especially true for people who had grown up in the regions most impacted. The research suggests that in parts of the world where natural disasters are a more common part of life, people are not as surprised by them. Therefore, they demonstrate capacities to experience, process, grieve, and ultimately integrate disaster into their lives with fewer long-term mental health issues.

In a word, they are resilient.

The people of Indonesia don't have some superhuman capacity to muscle up and double down in the face of devastation. What they have are (a) deep connections to each other, and (b) sober expectations that tough stuff is part of life. Because natural disasters are part of what it means to be alive, when disasters like the earthquake and tsunami come, they have a mental paradigm that helps them make sense of it. To them, it isn't an unimaginable tragedy. Again, this doesn't mean the events of 2004 weren't devastating, just not categorically shocking.

They'd come to expect the unexpected.

To embrace the unfiguroutable . . . together.

The same belonging that equips us to tolerate the liminality of devastation also shapes our sense of purpose. Eleventh-century French mystic Bernard of Clairvaux says, "A canal simultaneously pours out what it receives; the reservoir retains the water till it is filled, then discharges the overflow without loss to itself."[21] If we invest in positive, loving, mutual relationships, the contents of those relationships might become the reservoir of our lives.

When we see our purpose as overly individualistic, we miss the bigger picture of what God is doing. Then we fall prey to the untenable pressure that we have to be the superheroes of our own story or anyone else's. The reality is we simply can't. Even if we come to expect the unexpected, we're still only human. We still need each other. The bond of the community is one of love.

Love Helps Us Find Our Way Home

Patrick Reyes once interviewed me for his podcast, and his opening question was one I'll never forget: "Who loved you into being?"

I've heard him say elsewhere that he's cultivated a practice of reorienting himself to love, particularly by recalling the folks who, like my own grandma did for me, had his back no matter what. Whether these folks are living or dead, with us or not, tapping into that love orients us toward home in that it orients us toward them, our longings, and who we really are deep down.[22]

Several years ago, long after Grandma passed away, I became increasingly curious about how good leaders are formed. Not just the folks who put up big numbers or launch innovative products but the people others want to follow. The people others see as healthy. While my pursuit of this question has been nuanced and not the core focus of this book, there's a point that's worth noting here: relationships play a profound role in the formation of good leaders.

Take Aaron, for example. When we met Aaron, he had a successful career leading a large retail vertical for a rapidly growing technology company. Growing up, he had an older brother, Tre, who was good in school. Tre got a scholarship to college, which really set the tone for what Aaron expected of himself. He got a scholarship too, but he lost it because his grades were bad. Eventually, he had to move back home. When he did, he joined the business of a family friend. But, in part due to a bad call Aaron made, they lost some big contracts, and the business went down. From there, he grew distant from his family.

One day, he quite literally hit rock bottom. After an argument with his spouse, he had nowhere to go. With only the clothes on his back, he walked the six miles across the suburbs of Chicago to his mom's house—both a place he felt ashamed to return to and one where he knew deep down he was loved no matter what. She welcomed him with wide arms and made a place for him at her table. She told him to remain there until he was recentered, had healed, had made restitution, and was back on his feet. All he wanted was clarity about what he should do next, but his mom's instructions were firm: just remain here.

It's as simple and as complicated as this for us too. In order for our lives to bear the fruit we imagine is possible, we must remain in Christ and in trusted, loving relationships. Christ dwells in the collective us, and so we also must dwell in the collective us. We need to remain with each other in the fog.

Now, let's be very clear. Lisa and I are not suggesting you stay in relationships that are unsafe. You are not required to lean in when others treat you poorly. This is true for romantic relationships, relatives, friends, mentors, pastors—anyone, really. Even the best and safest relationships are hard. There's hurt, misunderstanding, and betrayal. Forgiveness and tough conversations are needed, but staying in a relationship that harms you is not at all what we're advocating for.

The mutuality of relationships is messy. People hurt.

The search to make sense of ourselves is ultimately a spiritual quest—a homecoming, if you will. But in an age when everything feels in flux and we cannot feel the tethers of home, our search is made both more urgent and more difficult.

When we are making our way, bit by bit, through the fog, the Christian message remains very good news: we are God's beloved beings. Grenz writes, "Because we are the creatures of God, we can know both where we come from and where we are going."[23]

In God, we find both the home we came from and the home to which we are ultimately destined. And in those bookends, we can begin to make sense of who we are. While this is ultimately comforting, it can create tension in the now. Home isn't just a place out there with God; it is a place right here with God and others.

In Wendell Berry's beloved *Jayber Crow*, he writes:

> And so I came to belong to this place. . . . Being here satisfies me. I had laid my claim on the place, had made it answerable to my life. Of course, you can't do that and get away free. You can't choose, it seems, without being chosen. For the place, in return, had laid its claim on me and had made my life answerable to it.[24]

Some of us think of a physical place as home. But in an increasingly mobile world, more and more people think of home as a space. What does home mean in a world that's in flux? For this book, Lisa and I asked nearly a hundred people how they defined *home*. Common to their answers was the way they felt and who helped make them feel that way. As the world moves faster, and more of life is disorienting, home is a space in which we are known, loved, and valued. Home is a space in which others love us not only into being but into mature and fruitful disciples. Home is a space where bravery comes and peace abounds. Home can handle hard questions because, at home, we're never alone. Home is a place where we don't have to think about being ourselves. We don't have to impress anyone. It's where we are the most comfortable and where we feel the most loved.

We long for home when we're feeling inadequate or uncomfortable.

We long for it when we're feeling lost or sad.

We turn toward it when the fog settles in.

In this, we are accountable to home—to the spaces made up of people who value us and love us deeply. To these spaces, we owe something. We owe our affection, our care, our honesty, our vulnerability, and our growth. Curt Thompson, in discussing with Tish Harrison Warren why burnout has become such a prevalent part of modern life, says, "We know that the brain can do a lot of really hard things for a long time, as long it doesn't have to do them by itself. We only develop greater resilience when we are deeply emotionally connected to other people."[25]

When we navigate the way forward together, we can do powerful things. We see evidence of this on elite sports teams. Psychologist Gier Jodet has studied the penalty kick shootout in World Cup Soccer. His study is fascinating, and there is much to be gleaned from his work. What stood out to Lisa and me was this:

> But shootouts are team sports disguised as individual confrontations. There is an emotional contagion in which the mere reactions of players can shape the events on the field—for good and bad. . . . Teammates can make it less lonely. Communicate. Talk. Be present for others. Move. Interact. . . . This is far more productive than standing still and quiet, which is what many teams do.[26]

It turns out that being a supportive colleague matters as much on the soccer field as in the office. In all spaces and places, we need others. In the hard times, we need colleagues, partners, and team members who join us in the fog and are willing to struggle with us as we navigate through it.

Moving through life in flux isn't a solo project; it's communal work.

Belonging Shapes Our Choices

Our belonging reshapes our vision of home and what we long for deep down. Take, for instance, Jack, who is a senior vice president of sales at a major automotive group. He discovered that one of his company's most popular cars had an engine defect that, while not enough to render the car inoperable, could end up costing owners hundreds of dollars annually in maintenance fees. The engine would not likely last as long as owners expected, given the historical reliability of the brand. Because he cared so much about these customers and did not want to burden them with additional costs related to owning this car, he asked the company to pause manufacturing and sales until they could address the defect in the engine.

Because of the popularity of this car model, Jack's decision put at risk both the company's profits and the income of salespeople who were paid on commission. Some top-performing salespeople actually left the company, opting for workplaces where they wouldn't miss a beat in racking up sales. But the ones who chose to stay did so because, like Jack, they didn't feel right about putting a subpar product on the market. The fact that their leadership would place individual lives above profitability ended up making these employees loyal to the company in a way that Jack had not predicted. Though it took a couple of years, this values-driven sales team ended up shattering sales records that more than made up for the short-term loss in profit.[27]

> **COMMON POSTURE:** I look past the people right in front of me as I (impatiently) await a sign from God on what I should do or how I move next.
>
> **UNCOMMON POSTURE:** I move empathetically toward the people right in front of me.

In this case, deep care for the customer led to lasting and meaningful results. Of course, that isn't always how it works. Sometimes we care deeply for people and still end up shortchanged or heartbroken. That's very real. Sometimes we work for or with people who are anything but healthy, leaving us powerless even when we can see the way forward. Unfortunately, caring isn't a sure bet. It can feel pretty risky.

That's why we have to honestly decide if we will take that risk. Are we willing to care for others and let them care for us? In order to answer that question, we have to understand our context and whether people are safe enough to hold our care. We have to understand who we can truly belong to.

It seems to me that as the world speeds up and things seem more chaotic, we can't help but want to hoard enough resources for ourselves. We live in an age that tells us we can do anything and be anything we want. But the hidden message is that we've got to pull it off ourselves. We've got to shore up our walls so that we'll be okay.

Unfortunately, when things go wrong, that means we have only ourselves to blame.

Building relationships is difficult, especially as we get older. That's why we need some tools to consider who is on our boat. We need to find a way to know who our people are, to recognize those we truly belong with.

One way to visualize how we relate to different people is to picture them on our boat. We can think of the few who fall into our inner core as our *trusted crew*. The ones we'll turn to first when the fog rolls in. These are the people whom we trust to tell us the truth even when it hurts. The people who love us and are for us. Most of us have just a few people in our trusted crew, maybe two or three.

Then our *teammates* are the people we have solid connections with and are aligned with on many things. We may work toward common goals together. These people are trusted advisers in certain areas but not all areas of our lives.

We also have *passengers*, who are a larger group of friends and acquaintances we have things in common with but are not in our innermost circles. At least not yet! They may move there over time. We can think about the parent we see every day at school drop-off or the colleague who is on another team but we always enjoy having a conversation with. These are people who might like our Instagram posts or come to a milestone birthday, but they're not in the weeds of our everyday lives.

Finally, there are the *people on the shore*. These are the people we occasionally encounter but have no real established connection with. Think about the people we meet at a conference, or someone whose work we admire from afar, or the neighborhood council president we've never said more than hello to.

These groups are not static, and people may enter our inner circles or leave them over time. No matter what, we really do need them, each and every one, in our lives. At every level, human connection is important for making our way through a life in flux. We are hardwired for intimacy—the kind of intimacy where we are with a person who knows us so well that we are home with them. This kind of intimacy sustains us in seasons of disorientation and disruption.

**The
Intimate 3**
High Trust/Vulnerability

The Collaborative 12
Medium Trust/Vulnerability

The Enjoyable Crew
Limited Trust/Vulnerability

The Unknowable Crowd
Friendly, Low Trust/Vulnerability

A Prayer for My Trusted Crew

Two in a bed warm each other.
Alone, I shiver all night.
By myself, I'm unprotected.
With a friend, I can face the worst.
Can I round up a third?
A three-stranded rope isn't easily snapped.

Oh my God,
here I am again,
all alone.

The weight of trying to go it solo
is literally killing me.

I need help.

Help me to see the people who can be trusted,
to invite them in,
even as I feel exposed and vulnerable.

To be with me, and I with them.
To help me pause and listen,
to discern the next steps.
To bear the pain together,
to cry hallelujah arm in arm.
To petition you for each other.
To help me feel at home, even in the fog.

Amen.

Stay in
Your Headlights

I love strategy. It's my top skill on a myriad of different personality tests. (Remember, I am the person who takes them all!) As the leader of a small organization nestled within a larger one, I've been told that we should do more long-range strategic planning, and maybe someday we will. But for now, it's hard to find value in five-year strategic plans. In my experience, the world just moves too fast. There's too much on the horizon. Things have changed and continue to change. And with a small team that's relatively nimble, that level of detailed planning feels like wasted energy we can't afford.

I'm not alone. In the workforce, traditional strategic planning is being replaced with a more iterative process. People are growing comfortable with a ten-year vision and a one-year plan. Where do we envision we might be in a decade? And what small steps do we need to take to move in that direction?

This approach is helpful for life in flux. It's natural to want to architect the whole picture and move methodically toward a destination on the horizon, and if that works for us, great. But more often than not, because of the way disruption disorients us along the way, our visibility is much more limited. Because things are foggy, we cannot see the horizon.

Twentieth-century American novelist E. L. Doctorow talked about his writing this way: "Writing is like driving at night in the fog. You can only see as far as your headlights, but you can make the whole trip that way."[1] And so it should be for our process of moving through life in flux. We can make our whole way by staying in our headlights, moving bit by bit toward where we long to go.

NAVIGATIONAL SKILL #8:

Stay in Your Headlights

I operate within limits for the sake of my forward movement.

Learning to stay in our headlights can be one of the most stretching of any of the Navigational Skills.[2] It requires us to recognize what's actually ours to do in any given situation and, conversely, what is not.

We can come to know what's in our headlights a variety of ways. Partly, it is the natural limitations we all have as humans, the "only so many hours in a day" kind of stuff. But it's context too—our job description, our family of origin, our sociocultural location. And it's also something deeper. It's our sense of God's calling along with our sense of identity—both who we are and who we are not, deep down inside.

A Can-Do Space

If we are competent people who have delivered results, the environments we operate in will often push us very hard to build more skills, take on more responsibility, and work mostly outside of our core strengths. Think of this as a can-do space. If something is in the can-do space, it's something we have the capacity to do, yes, but it's not necessarily aligned with our intrinsic motivation. Once we start doing a particular skill or task and do it well, people want to rely on us to do it more and more. The problem is that just because we *can* do something doesn't mean we *should.*

I once was on a retreat at a sacred place of reflection and renewal set to the backdrop of mountains and a rushing river. I was there to teach, but honestly, I was the one learning. I had just come off a season of work in which I was completely overextended. I had been traveling too much, and on so many levels I was paying the price for saying yes to too many things at the same time as I was transitioning professional roles.

Yes, I had been operating way outside my headlights.

Fueled by my strategic thinking and deep care for people, more times than I care to admit, I've assumed responsibility for other people's problems. And I end up not only solving problems no one ever asked me to deal with but also being completely overextended in my own life. It happens so fast. I dive all in, and before I know it, I'm driving in the dark, bumping up against all sorts of obstacles along the way.

On the heels of that very tough season, then, I was now coming face-to-face with some hard lessons about what was actually mine to do.

While on that retreat, I went on a solo hike that promised a grand lookout over the river. As I made my way up the handholds on a section of boulders, I passed over a lanyard with a name tag attached. It was Bob's, a new friend of mine from the retreat. As I bent over to scoop it up, I sensed very clearly that this was not my work to do. That's right. I *sensed* that I wasn't supposed to pick up Bob's lanyard. Odd as it sounds, I put it back on the ground and kept walking.

This simple act was hard for me because—as noted—I am a compulsive problem solver. At dinner that night, I told Bob exactly where he could find his lanyard. He looked at me, part bewildered and part annoyed. And rightfully so. *Trust me, Bob, it would have been way easier for me had I just picked it up!* My cheeks hot with embarrassment, I awkwardly explained to him that I had sensed it wasn't mine to do, which honestly was such a weird thing to say to someone I hardly knew about a lanyard out on the trail.

The next morning, Bob came up to me at breakfast. He wanted to show me a video. It was from earlier that morning when he had gone out to retrieve his name tag. In the video, two young black bears scampered around, delighting in morning play on the banks of the river. Birds sang in the background, and I could hear Bob oohing and aahing in the foreground. He told me that his time that morning had been a deeply meaningful, sacred experience.

"I was actually really frustrated by you last night," he told me. "But this morning, I'm thankful for you."

If that isn't a metaphor for what God was teaching me, I don't know what is! It went against every impulse in my body to leave that lanyard lying on the rocks. But I was learning, in that small, low-stakes way, that not everything was mine to do.

As modern citizens, we are enculturated to do many things, often simultaneously, so it's easy to think we can and should do more than is really ours to do. Even the good stuff, like helping out a friend who left his lanyard on the trail. Sometimes it really is our work to drop everything and help. (Hello, the Good Samaritan!) But in a world in which we are increasingly connected, we simply have more exposure to more people's problems more often. This isn't meant to detach us from the pain of the world but only to say we have to be mindful about what we can actually do. We simply can't always be the one doing what needs to be done. There are limits to what we can do.

What Happens When We Don't Stay in Our Headlights

We previously touched on the first part of Lisa's story, in which she came face-to-face with a series of limiting beliefs that were impacting her life, work, and leadership. That season of waking up and letting go enabled her to dig deep and ultimately lead the organization in a complete turnaround effort. The only problem? Because Lisa was so adept at problem-solving, the system grew to function around her even as it drained the life from her. Gifted at making change happen, speaking prophetically and directly, and shaping things upfront, Lisa had skills that were great for such a turnaround effort. But following that period, she struggled with some of the skills needed to steward a growing nonprofit organization.

As the pace of work picked up, Lisa found herself regularly functioning outside of her most natural and coherent gifting. She was routinely operating well outside of her headlights. She wasn't sleeping well. She felt scattered. Doctors told her that her body wasn't in good shape. She was holding too much stress in her body over too long a period of time. She was overextended and not functioning on all cylinders, expending enormous energy on tasks and requirements that were, at best, needs she could meet but not core to her gifts and strengths.

Eventually, she became burned out.

Unfortunately, *burnout* is an increasingly normal word in today's world. On the topic, sisters Emily and Amelia Nagoski wrote *Burnout: The Secret to Unlocking the Stress Cycle*. Drawing on the work of psychologist Herbert Frudenberger, they describe burnout as having three components: emotional exhaustion, depersonalization, and decreased sense of accomplishment. In a podcast interview with the sisters, Brené Brown paraphrases their definitions in this helpful way:

1. **Emotional exhaustion**: the fatigue that comes from caring too much for too long.
2. **Depersonalization**: the depletion of empathy, caring, and compassion.
3. **Decreased sense of accomplishment**: the unconquerable sense of futility, feeling that nothing you do makes any difference.[3]

Caring too much for too long. Running out of empathy or care to offer yourself or others. Feeling like nothing you do will matter. Ever been there?

In Lisa's case, she was carrying too much of the wrong thing while caring so deeply for too long. She was deeply invested in the work itself while exhausted by the requirements of the CEO role. And when we, like Lisa, operate outside of our headlights for a sustained period of time, burnout is a likely scenario.

In *Let Your Life Speak*, Parker Palmer writes:

> Though usually regarded as the result of trying to give too much, burnout in my experience results from trying to give what I did not possess—the ultimate in giving too little! Burnout is a state of emptiness, to be sure, but it does not result from giving all I have: it merely reveals the nothingness from which I was trying to give in the first place.[4]

So, why do so many of us feel that we've got to take on more than really is possible? How did we get here? In *The Burnout So-*

ciety, Byung-Chul Han argues that, as a society, we've replaced traditional values of discipline and self-control with positivity and self-improvement. A society that values positivity and self-improvement above all else becomes a pressure cooker for striving to do more—to make it all happen. Pair that with technological tools that facilitate our round-the-clock availability and subsequent greater capacity to be productive, and it's no wonder so many of us spend so much time so regularly outside our headlights. Under the cover of excess positivity, our drive for productivity and results lands us in a state of complete exhaustion.[5]

Our recalibration comes through a healthy dose of reality, self-regulation, and ongoing discipline.

Getting clear.

Saying no.

Paring back.

Setting down the work that demands something we never possessed.

COMMON POSTURE: There is a need; I have to meet it whatever it takes.

UNCOMMON POSTURE: There are some needs I am best suited to meet; I focus on those.

Of course, this isn't just an individual issue. It's systemic too. In her story, it wasn't just Lisa who was suffering. The organization was also hurting as relational connections splintered and the board, staff, and Lisa grew to be misaligned. It was a system that encouraged people to overproduce and neglect their own limits. And Lisa was part of the problem.

While Lisa could continue in the leadership role of the organization, she was at an inflection point. The organization faced a new season of change and challenge, and she had to come to terms with the fact that she simply was not made for and had no desire to pursue what it would require of her. In fact, many of the requirements for a highly effective nonprofit CEO, while within her competencies, were a real energy drain for her, including building an effective fundraising engine and driving the real change needed on the board. She had to acknowledge that, after her extended season of operating outside her headlights, both the organization and she needed something different.

When Lisa was in the thick of trying to figure out how to rein it all in and if she should stay on at all, a wise counselor asked her a critical question: "Are you staying as the CEO out of fear, guilt, or obligation?"

Oof. What a gut punch. She knew it wasn't fear or guilt. But obligation? That truth stung. She sensed that her patterns of overextension had a lot to do with her rescuing tendencies. She felt obligated to meet needs and expectations, even if doing so caused her to overextend herself in unhealthy ways. Faced with the truth and completely drained physically, emotionally, relationally, and spiritually, Lisa did the only thing left to do: she resigned.

It is human nature to bend ourselves toward the expectations of others and to project a positive version of who we think we ought to be. A helpful problem solver. A heroic leader. A (fill in the blank). This version of ourselves that we project is just that: a projection. It is not entirely coherent with who we are deep down. Part of why we operate outside of our headlights is that we do not know ourselves in the deepest sense. As a result, we don't know what is ours and what isn't.

Our projected self is sometimes the only part of ourselves we allow people to see. We've referred to this already as the stage mask we put on. We don't have manipulative intent; we've just learned how to be a certain way in front of others, and this false self becomes second nature. The version of ourselves that we present to the world might help to insulate us from pain and be the version of ourselves we think we ought to be. Sometimes, because the systems of the world are so obviously not built for us, it's almost as if the world demands our false selves and pushes our true selves to the side. If this is our experience, chances are it's cost us a great deal.

Often, coming to understand the shape of our headlights doesn't mean we can walk away from responsibility. It also doesn't mean we're now on a quest to find a perfect job or a new self. It does mean that God intends for us to be coherent people. One person, in all our beauty and brokenness, in every place we are called to belong.

To get to this true self, we must do all the work that is ours to do over the course of a lifetime. In fact, that is what contemplative theologians suggest *is* the work of a lifetime. While in one sense this work will always be undone, through it we can come to know ourselves deeply and gain a stronger sense of what is ours to do.

In contrast, the more we work out of the shadows of ourselves—the projections of personality we have carefully crafted for the world to see—the more we risk creating the kind of collateral damage that wreaks havoc on both ourselves and those around us.

The cultural mantra we hear often, especially in self-improvement spaces, is this: *become the best possible version of yourself.* And while we do want to grow as followers of Jesus, approaching self-improvement in a "more is better" kind of way only puts us back on the achievement track. It's not about accumulating lots of great versions of our self; it's about excavating to uncover our unique, only self. This is what gives shape to how we move through the world and what is actually ours to do.

This is what enables us to release what is way outside of our headlights.

How We Stay in Our Headlights

Discernment is slow work that only gets slower when the fog rolls in. This means we won't benefit from quick fixes but rather need sustainable rhythms that help us go the distance as we listen courageously and coherently to the shape of our own lives. Lisa and I have identified five specific strategies that help us to focus on what's in our headlights. Though we'll move through them individually here, keep in mind they're interdependent. We really can't do one without doing the others if we want to find a way forward in the flux.

1. Be intentional.

Remember Stacey, the accountant wrestling with whether or not she wanted to be a partner? When Stacey launched her career, her *intention* was to be a top-performing accountant. She loved numbers and cared deeply for people. In her estimation, being an accountant was the perfect way to care for people by helping them with their numbers. She set her *attention* on building technical competencies. She wanted to be the most helpful she could be. Which is why, at first, when the possibility of partner came up, she said no because it didn't fit her goals.

After she turned down the opportunity, one of her mentors asked her a critical question: "What do you want for yourself in this next season?"

COMMON POSTURE: What do I want from myself and others?

UNCOMMON POSTURE: What do I want for myself and others?

We're good at asking ourselves what we want *from* ourselves, right? *From* sets us up for more accomplishments, achievements, and goals. More to-dos. We're not always as seasoned at asking what we want *for* ourselves. *For* elicits a different response. It's about intention, longing, and desire.

When the possibility of becoming a partner came up, Stacey realized she didn't yet have the leadership experience needed to help lead an organization. However, she realized she actually did want that *for* herself. When she sat with the tough questions, she recognized she had a deep desire to help lead the company into the future. So, she recalibrated her intention toward that end.

Her *intention* focused her *attention*. No longer was she solely prioritizing technical competencies. Now she sought to grow as a leader of people. That meant she had to come to know herself and get comfortable with the fog (among other things!). As she pressed into the disorientation and worked with a coach, she realized there were some parts of herself she wasn't currently using at work—namely the part of her that planned family vacations. Every year, she would plan and organize an adventurous trip for fifteen members of her extended family. They'd visit a national park or camp out near the ocean. They'd tour museums and eat at delicious hole-in-the-wall restaurants. Stacey loved planning those trips! So much so that she wondered if there was a way to bring this adventurous leader in herself to the table as part of her path forward.

Adventure at an accounting firm? Stacey knew that whatever she did would still have to be intelligent, measured, and responsible. But she also knew that if she was going to embrace more leadership, it would have to be in an adventurous way. She talked with the partners about leading a project around discovering the firm's core values in order to help them consider who they wanted to be as a firm in a rapidly changing world. When she set her intention on the adventure of helping the accounting firm make its way into the future, she focused her attention on a process for doing that. Then, her energy followed.

One way to stay in our headlights is by doing the same. No, this doesn't mean we all plan adventurous excursions for our families or lead our coworkers down a path of wonder and discovery (though that would be fun!). I mean we have to focus on intention. We have to stay in the habit of regularly naming what our intention is.

I want to connect more deeply with my children.

I want to grow in the Ignatian spiritual practices.

I want to help the people I manage to get promoted.

Whatever it is, setting that intention helps guide our attention toward it. It helps us find our way forward in the right direction for us when the fog settles in.

2. Lean on the wisdom of a trusted crew.

As we grow more accustomed to recognizing when we're outside of our headlights, the question that resurfaces time and time again to ask ourselves is this: *What is mine to do?* Sometimes the answer is clear, and other times it's not at all clear. That's where the wisdom of trusted others in our lives can help.

When Lisa and I touched on this topic previously, we encouraged you to identify the people who are in your boat. Knowing who these people are and what role they play in your life is very important, not only for knowing where your deepest connections come from but also for the work of staying in your headlights. These are the people who know you and want the best *for* you. They're the ones willing to call you on the carpet when you're wrong.

We are all prone to absorb opinions and feedback from people who are way outside of our inner circle. There are, of course, scenarios where this makes sense—a boss gives us feedback or our kids' teacher brings up something the entire family needs to attend to. But sometimes the feedback comes from what some might call the cheap seats. Beloved author Brené Brown repopularized an oft-used quote from President Teddy Roosevelt in her book *Dare to Lead*. Brown said:

> If you are not in the arena getting your a— kicked on occasion, I am not interested in or open to your feedback. There are a million cheap seats in the world today filled with people who will never be brave with their lives but who will spend every ounce of energy they have hurling advice and judgment at those who dare greatly. Their only contributions are criticism, cynicism, and fear-mongering. If you're criticizing from a place where you're not also putting yourself on the line, I'm not interested in what you have to say.[6]

If someone isn't daring enough to enter the ring themselves or hasn't done the work to grow Navigational Skills suited for the fog, then we might want to consider how much of their feedback we take in. Hear it, consider it, and listen for the truth in it? Sure. Give it ongoing space in our hearts and minds? Maybe not. Proverbs 27 tells us, "Wounds from a friend can be trusted, but an enemy multiplies kisses" (v. 6). Feedback is crucial to our growth, but receiving it from someone we trust is paramount.

We must consider whose feedback we take to heart. Who has permission to speak truth into our lives, even when it is painful and hard to hear? Having a close group of no more than three or four people who make up our *wisdom council* is vital if we are to do the work of staying in our headlights with integrity. These are the people who can be deeply trusted, who know us well, and who have permission to say hard things to us when necessary. They can be relied on when they see us stretching beyond our headlights to ask us the question, "Is that really yours to do?"

When we're in the fog, trying to process something difficult, or unsure about whether or not something is ours to do, we can invite our wisdom council to ask us the following questions:

- What are you not seeing in this situation that you need to be aware of?
- What do you need to own?
- What do you need to release?

Having a group of people who will be lovingly and relentlessly honest with us is one of the greatest gifts in life. This trusted crew may include a spouse or partner, a dear friend or two, a trusted parent, and a counselor, spiritual director, or coach. Do not wait until there is a crisis to assemble them. Invite them into your life when the waters are calm and invest in each other with the promise that, when you face difficult decisions and hard challenges, they will be in the boat with you—and vice versa.

3. Stay present to the present.

In an age when so many things compete for our attention and energy, we find ourselves in a crisis of attention. If we don't know what to pay attention to in the small things, how will we ever discern what to do when things change? What the world needs is more people who are awake—awake to the problems of the world and the issues in our own lives. If waking up puts us on the journey, *staying* awake sustains it.

I once was at a baseball game with my two kids, then ages four and seven. My young son asked for M&Ms, and I obliged. As he scampered toward the candy machine, he momentarily went out of sight. I thought, *It's ok, he'll be at the M&Ms.* Still, I picked up my pace to catch up.

When I got to the M&Ms not two seconds later, he wasn't there. He'd been swallowed by the crowd of twenty-five thousand people and was nowhere in sight. I scanned the area, and when I didn't see him, I went straight for the nearest exit. I systematically alerted all the workers there not to let a small redheaded boy out while I simultaneously deployed my older daughter to check all the VIP rooms.

Nowhere.

The minutes ticked on, and my heart started to really race. My problem-solving instincts that told me he had to be somewhere close by gave way to the fear rising in my chest. More minutes went by with still no sign of him. Half a dozen employees were searching. I trusted my daughter would keep her eye on me, and I started to run.

Finally, I saw him.

He was being escorted toward me by a couple. I heard the man say to my son, "You're ok. Chin up, buddy. Don't worry." When he saw me, he started sprinting my way. As he did, my fear turned to anger. How could he run off like that? In that moment between when I saw him and when I reached him, I looked up at the woman who was with him. She met my eye knowingly, her look compassionate enough to hold my pain.

We tell the crying child they will be okay. We lash out at each other when we are afraid. But rarely are we awake enough to look each other deeply in the eye and hold space for each other's pain. That woman's confidence melted my anger, so much so that, by the time my son got to me, I was ready to kneel down and hold him as he wept, and I was able to tell him, "You must have been so scared. I was too."

I never even said thank you to that woman, but she didn't need me to. She was so awake to the moment—so aware of what was hers to do—that she didn't need a single thing more from anyone. And my goodness, was she a whole sermon about staying awake to the present when disorientation sets in!

Our ability to attend to what matters most is one part courage and another part practice. One part calibration to God in any given moment and another part willingness to embrace that which we so commonly deem dark. When we fall asleep to our own lives, we stray from our headlights. We have to stay present to the present. It's then that we're more prone to be guided by the light.

4. Work within constraints.

Of course, even as we set our intentions, we have to be mindful of our constraints, which are the resources we have access to that shape what's possible, like time, money, relationships, and ideas.

When I first had children, I wrestled with how to think about my roles as a mother and as a professional. A woman whose work I admire and who is also the mother of four gave me advice that I'll never forget. She told me that the most valuable lesson she learned while on maternity leave with her first child was that she was, in fact, replaceable in her job.

At first, that sounded harsh to me, and contrary to the idea that she was special and significant. But as I listened more deeply, she described how coming face-to-face with the reality that she was not indispensable or superhuman in her work was ultimately liberating. She did not have to do it all. She would never do it all. She should not try to do it all. She was not the only one who could do great work. She was free to live inside the limits of her humanity—to operate with excellence within the natural constraints of her life.

When she told me that story, her kids were in their teenage years, and she was at the top of her field as a respected professional who was doing really amazing work. So, I decided to believe her. She helped me to see that the way to make our way through a challenging season is to work within constraints, not outrun them.

Constraints are the guardrails that keep us on track and, more specifically, in our lane. If we truly lean in to them, we'll have seasons where we actually move rather fast. Constraints on their own aren't a mandate to go slow but rather to be focused. There are times when focusing means slowing down, but other times focusing enables greater speed. The problem is that most of us do not operate inside constraints. As a result, we don't know when to go fast or slow, and we end up moving at a pace that ultimately feels unproductive.

Unfortunately, the white, Western narrative has specifically misled us when it comes to constraints. We have been taught that anything is possible. We can be anything we want to be. We can do whatever it is we set our minds on. These things simply aren't true or ideal. We have very real limits as humans, and those limits are part of what makes us human. The narratives that push over-production, overconsumption, and grinding it out at every turn simply don't have a solid grasp on what it means to be human.[7]

Sometimes our limitations feel more like "thorns in the flesh" than good gifts from God. The apostle Paul writes this to the Corinthians on the matter:

> Therefore, in order to keep me from becoming conceited, I was given a thorn in my flesh, a messenger of Satan, to torment me. Three times I pleaded with the Lord to take it away from me. But he said to me, "My grace is sufficient for you, for my power is made perfect in weakness." (2 Cor. 12:7–9)

We have talked at length about knowing ourselves and operating from a place of giftedness and strength. But it's also important to acknowledge that we all have weaknesses, and God can and does work through them. In fact, getting clear-eyed about our individual weaknesses—our own constraints—helps us notice the work of God and lean on others even more.

5. Clarify values.

Beyond the really practical resources, such as time or money, there are more intangible constraints. These include our values. Our values are what matter most to us—what's important to us in crisis and good times alike. If the intention is *where*, then our values are *how* we get to where we want to go.

Values are both communal and individual. Chances are what we value is important to us because it's also important to others. When we truly share values with people, it's a powerful compass for the way forward. And in that, values, especially shared ones, give shape to how we arrange our everyday lives. They become the measure for decision-making when the stakes and emotions get high.

Juanita had finished her MBA and had several strong leads on a job, the most exciting of which was with one of the most prestigious consulting firms in the country. It was her dream job, really. She was also weeks away from a move to the city where her fiancé was located. There, he was coparenting his two young children with his ex-wife.

As the consulting prospect started to crystallize, she realized the dream job would require her to work in a city nine hundred miles from where she would be living with her new husband. The company wanted her to fly in on Sunday nights and fly out on Friday nights for forty-plus weeks of the year.

She was torn. Should she take the dream job and hope she might be able to transfer to her home city in the future? Or say no and give up that dream?

She sought input from her trusted crew, who asked her several important questions:

- What really matters most to you?
- What are the values you have defined for yourself over the last few years?

- What have you and your future husband discerned you want for your marriage?

In the end, she turned down the job. She and her fiancé had agreed together that they would support one another's career ambitions wholeheartedly, and they would always make one another and their blended family a top priority, especially in the early years of their marriage. Juanita wept over the lost opportunity but also felt relieved. She knew herself well enough to know that this kind of travel schedule would have cost everyone too much. She would have been way outside of her headlights in a season of impending flux, and that would serve no one well.

What is true for individuals is also true for organizations. Values get traction when a group has articulated what each value looks like in very simple, concrete behaviors. For example, a team might value respect, which can mean lots of different things. One of the behaviors that they put in place to support this value could be something like, "We don't schedule back-to-back meetings, knowing we each need breathing space between meetings to recover and be able to show up prepared." This helps them demonstrate respect: they give each other the space to show up as their best selves, from both a screen time and a preparation standpoint.

The more well-defined our values are, the more helpful they are in moments of disruption. If we've said out loud what we believe and know that we actually mean it, values can ground us and give us a sense of clarity when the seas get rough. In the midst of a volatile situation or a complex decision like Juanita's, we don't want to be trying to decide what our values are. We need to already have them set. If we do, they will guide us where we need to go—even if they guide us to hard or unpopular decisions.

One night, during the height of tax season, Stacey walked into the office of one of the junior accountants, Chris. In the accounting world, tax season is huge. You work long hours and late nights, and there's very little rest. For a few weeks, Chris had been growing more and more weary. That night he looked exhausted, and Stacey suspected he'd reached the point of being unproductive. So, she did something counterintuitive. She told him to take two days off.

Completely off.

No laptop. No client emails. Nothing.

She redistributed his work and took as much as she could herself.

It is absolutely unheard of to take two solid days off in late March in the accounting world, right? Why did Stacey do it?

In her work of leading the company through a process of clarifying who they were, the team had many conversations about how the firm might remain an institution that offered a truly valuable service in a changing world. As part of this, they did a lot of values work. One of the values that rose to the top was *extraordinary care* for clients.

As Stacey watched Chris push himself to the point of complete exhaustion, she knew there would be no way he could provide extraordinary care for clients if he wasn't cared for extraordinarily by the firm. Though her offer to Chris was unprecedented, she knew exactly what to do, because she was able to align the next steps with the company's stated values. In this case, staying in her headlights meant doing something brand-new.

And it worked—twofold. Not only did it show Chris his value but it helped Stacey find a new sense of adventure (something she longed for) in her role. Now she was able to realize that she loved caring for people in a way that felt adventurous, and that would suffice for her.

Because we are enculturated to put our heads down and just keep going harder, we often miss the moments when we're outside of our headlights and need to recalibrate. Stacey let company values guide her. She helped Chris recalibrate too. This was the right decision, even if it was an uncommon one.

As we embrace the reality that trying to do everything gets in the way of trying to do anything, we build confidence and courage to live within the limits of our humanity.

Disruptions are inevitable. Putting guardrails in place that help us stay in our headlights makes it easier to stay focused when uncertainty sets in. Intentionality is key. The wisdom and guidance of a few trusted crewmates can remind us of what we want *for* ourselves, what we intend, and what our values require of us.

Life in flux is a lot like driving at night in the fog. We can see only as far as our headlights. But the good news is that, if we are focused on what we need to do and what only we can do, we can make the entire trip home this way.

A Prayer for Staying in My Headlights

I confess that the fog scares me
and that I am outside my headlights before I even know it.

You are so gracious with me.

Hold me tight and help me calm the
impulse to say yes,
the temptation to go along,
to keep up my pattern of over-functioning
or compulsive problem-solving.

Show me what to let go of.
Help me take deep breaths.
Help me focus
on what is mine to do.

Show me how freeing
staying within my headlights can be.
One step at a time.

When the fog comes,
enable me to trust you.
Help me to acknowledge the systems that do not seek
    my best
and to look for the crewmates who are already in my boat,
wanting goodness and love for me.

Remind me that I can make the whole journey this way.

Amen.

At Home in Flux

I have heard it said that when a woman has her first child, she dies and is reborn. In the process of becoming a mother, she both unravels and is rebuilt. For the first six months of my daughter's life, she never slept for more than an hour and a half at a time. Which means I went half a year mostly sleeping in ninety-minute stints. It was exactly as brutal as it sounds. For many new moms, the first several months are a near-constant and ever-changing onslaught of demands wrapped up in a teeny, tiny, instantly loved person.

When the fog sets in, it forms us. In life's transitions and changes, over and over again we are reborn in small, subtle ways. The hope is that, as we develop and integrate counterintuitive Navigational Skills, we might come to feel at home in flux—in the very ebb and flow that disrupts and shapes us. With humility and confidence, we can be grounded for the way forward.

Just as a new mother makes her way through the fog one day at a time, we, too, are being formed along the way. It's as William

Bridges says in his seminal book about transitions: "For transition is simply the way in which one's life moves on and unfolds."[1] Life unfolds and stuff happens. As it does, either we grow or we don't. Even when we sense our own rupture and repair are impending, we rarely have the luxury of cocooning as we await our transformation. It happens in real-time rhythms amid the choices of our everyday lives. And with the support of the people who love us and to whom we are accountable.

Still, it can be so hard to sustain focus on how God is forming us in the midst of flux. In an age when so many things compete for our attention and energy, we often find ourselves in a crisis of attention. If we don't know what to pay attention to in the small things, how will we ever discern what to do with the big things?

In light of this, what the world desperately needs is more people who are truly awake—awake to the problems of the world and the issues in our own lives. People who are awake to the work that needs to be done and resolved to focus our attention there so that we can make our way forward. If waking up initiates the journey from *here* to *there*, being at peace in the midst of flux sustains it.

> **COMMON POSTURE:** When the seas get foggy or rough, I revert to habits that help me numb and avoid.
>
> **UNCOMMON POSTURE:** When the seas get foggy or rough, I take a deep breath and trust that I can be at home in the midst of flux.

From There to Here

While we're surely cultivating skills that will enable us to navigate acute moments and seasons of disorientation, any sense of this work as lasting requires us to take the long view.[2] In this, we can navigate more comfortably between remembering the past, staying in the present, and embracing the future. This work of a lifetime enables us to move with greater courage between *here* and *there* and, just as importantly, from *there* to *here*. We take ourselves not only from where we are now to where we want to go but from what we imagine out there back to our present reality.

Perhaps one of the greatest limiting beliefs that works against our ability to be at home in flux, right this very moment, is the narrative that we can go anywhere we want to go, do anything we want to do, and be anything we want to be, including the best version of ourselves.

From the time we are very small, we are told that if we just work hard enough, we can do anything and be anything. The issue, as mentioned earlier, is that this just isn't true. That's not to say that Lisa and I don't believe in the amazing and wonderful potential within each of us, but not all of us are destined to be presidents or professional athletes. Central to making peace with the fog is recognizing and releasing the aspirations of our late adolescence and early career.

I wanted to be a judge.

I always thought I would be a famous actor.

I imagined having five kids with the spouse of my dreams.

I was so passionate about solving world hunger.

When we have dreamed up what *there* looks like but never really arrive in the way we imagine, we carry with us the weight of those unfulfilled expectations. That makes it hard to embrace the fog. Releasing helps us let go of the weight of those expectations, sometimes before we even pick it up! And as we release what never came to be, we become more awake to what is. We create new space for new hopes.

William Bridges writes, "The natural developmental pattern is not for people to keep the same dreams but to relinquish old dreams and generate new ones throughout their lifetimes."[3] Dan Allender takes it one step further, suggesting that

> God is not in the business of helping us achieve our dreams—even the good ones that involve sacrifice. God is most committed to dissolving and re-creating our dreams. . . . It is in the pursuit of our dreams that we encounter tragedy and meet deeper desires that only loss and heartache can reveal.[4]

What we desired when we first began dreaming is likely not the same as what we hope for when we seek to set our compass and come home to ourselves. This means that, to be at home in flux, we have to make peace with life as it is.

For many of us, there comes a very real moment when we have to release the version of our lives we wish we had and embrace the one we actually have. That's not to say we don't make small, meaningful, and regular changes that help us more closely calibrate ourselves to God's work in the world. In fact, this entire book has been about these kinds of small (also kind of big!) changes. It's only to say that when we are at home in the lives we are actually living, facing the ebbs and flows of life in flux becomes more possible.

Elaine was on her way to being the youngest female CEO in company history. A caring, steady, and clear-eyed leader, though she was far from perfect, she was made for the fog. The problem? Elaine never wanted to be a CEO. Naturally oriented toward the future, she had grown up imagining herself as a teacher. But as the child of parents who struggled to keep steady employment, she knew early on that her ability to contribute to the family would be through financial success. When the time came for college, Elaine chose the route that was most promising financially: marketing. She had a full ride to a nearby school and got a job right out of college. After that, she quickly rose to the top.

Though she was proud of the work she did and grateful that she made such good money, a part of Elaine was always pained that she never got to be a teacher. So, even as she became the youngest female CEO in company history, she was grieving what would never be. And she had to! If she wanted to make peace with where she was now—the *here*—she had to move on from where she thought she wanted to be.

For others of us, it's less about releasing what never came to be and more about making peace with work left undone. Remember Sean, who was pushed out of the work he helped create at a public institution? Because his transition out had been so dramatic and traumatic, he really wrestled with the fact that so much of his work was undone. Over time, he was able to articulate that God was indeed calling him in a different direction. But that clarity didn't erase the pain of unfinished work and unresolved tension with people who had once been his friends. In order to be at home in the flux, Sean had to make peace with what was undone.

Earlier, I referenced Pauline Boss, a professor and researcher who suggests that closure is a myth. This is even truer when what we need to grieve is ambiguous. Life in flux is inevitably a dance of rupture and repair, and therefore we will benefit from the expectation that grief is paramount to the liminality of our times. Because keeping our eye on grief is such a tall order, it's easy to instead spend our whole lives reacting to things we cannot control or get lost in what never was. But when we spend our energy in this way, we steal from our own capacity to anticipate the future. Instead, by grieving what *isn't* in the here and now, we can better focus on making peace with what is, both now and as we make our way forward.

Integration Matters, and So Does Practice

As we inevitably face any number of disruptions in our lives, integration matters, and so does practice. Wise and rigorous whole person practice. Spiritual formation teacher Dallas Willard says this:

> We can, by faith and grace, become like Christ by practicing the types of activities he engaged in, by arranging our whole lives around the activities he himself practiced in order to remain constantly at home in the fellowship of his Father.[5]

By attending to the different parts of our lives and arranging them in an integrated way to practice our Navigational Skills, we prepare for what lies ahead.

In Luke 8, Jesus is out on a boat with his disciples and falls asleep. While he's sleeping, a sudden and powerful wind sends the water raging around him, and the boat starts taking on water. Presumably afraid that their boat will be damaged and they will drown, the disciples wake Jesus. Jesus rebukes the wind and raging waters. The storm dies down and all is calm.

When I imagine this story, I wonder how in the world Jesus can sleep soundly in the midst of a raging sea. He possesses a divine calm and peace in the midst of total chaos.

This posture of peace in the midst of upheaval is a theme of Jesus's life. Whether calming the crowds, healing the sick, comforting his followers, casting out demons, or standing steady in the face of death, over and over again, Jesus stays calm.

I'll admit that I wish it were as easy for us. I wish we could just simply see Jesus calm the raging water of the world or ask him to lift the fog in our own lives. I wish that every single time, just like that, he would. But a world in flux promises to never completely be stable. So, though we can't practice rebuking the wind and raging waters, we can practice a kind of contentment in God that, when layered on top of other Navigational Skills, enables us to be calm even if the storm rages on.

> **COMMON POSTURE:** When the waters get rough, I hunker down and seek safety.
>
> **UNCOMMON POSTURE:** When the waters get rough, I press on in the sea and point myself into the waves, trusting God in the midst of the storm.

On a cold winter's day in January 2009, Captain Chesley "Sully" Sullenberger was piloting US Airways Flight 1549 from New York City to Charlotte. Just minutes after takeoff, the plane hit a flock of birds, resulting in double engine failure. Quickly realizing that the plane couldn't make it back to the airport, Sully made the extraordinary decision to land in the Hudson River, adjacent to Midtown Manhattan. Calmly and quickly, he successfully landed the plane, saving the lives of all 155 passengers and crew members on board.

Sully was hailed as a hero for his incredible piloting skills and his ability to keep his cool under immense pressure. His non-anxious posture and decision-making skills helped prevent tragedy. As stories about Captain Sully started to emerge, what came out was that it was his years of training and experience coupled with the investment of mentors and teachers that enabled a safe landing that January day. Not only that but the cool heads of his crew made the rescue possible as passengers quite literally stood on the wings of the plane awaiting safety.[6] Had the crew dipped into panic or become disconnected from the people entrusted to their care—physically or metaphorically—there might have been a different outcome.[7]

Willard puts it this way: "A successful performance at a moment of crisis rests largely and essentially upon the depths of a self wisely and rigorously prepared in the totality of its being—mind and body."[8] Captain Sully was almost sixty years old when he performed the "miracle on the Hudson." He had flown commercially for three decades and had been a fighter pilot before that. In other words, he had experience. He had honed his skills and learned how to integrate them. Plus, he had practiced. So much so that his experience very well might have made the difference between life and death.[9]

Captain Sully and his team would not have had the skills to land and evacuate that plane without years on the job. And as we try to find our way in the fog, we can't attune to the ringing of the bell buoys without being out at sea a time or two in practice. The only way we can get good enough at navigating flux is by getting in the boat and heading out on the water. By intentionally and wisely practicing going from *here* to *there* in the small, low-risk moments that, no doubt, shape how we show up when things get their toughest. Consider how our response to a client when they give us difficult feedback might ready us for when our spouse loses their job. Or imagine how letting go of the way a colleague's words affect us might equip us to communicate more wholeheartedly when our kids' school tells us they are bullying.

Learning to be at home in flux in one moment is inevitably practice for being at home in flux in another. When we notice in ourselves or through others that we are moving from panic to pause, from anxiety to anticipation, from distraction to presence, from fear to courage, or from knowledge to wisdom, we can grow in confidence that living our lives at home in flux is the only true way to move through this world.

In her book *Imaginable*, Jane McGonigal, a futurist and game designer, describes how she drew on neuroscience to develop a process for a group of leaders to look ten years into the future and, based on a set of prescribed conditions, craft plans and problem-solve around the kinds of issues that might arise.[10] She first ran this future simulation gaming experiment, called EVOKE, as a ten-week process in 2010, in which the following happened:

> Nearly twenty thousand players [showed] up to predict what actions they could take to help others during a complex outbreak of possible future global crises including a pandemic, extreme climate change, and a radical misinformation group happening at the same time. EVOKE ran for 10 weeks and each week a new compounding crisis was added to the mix.[11]

Sound eerily familiar? As you read through the list of compounding crises, you will see that it was indeed prescient. Her simulation included a misinformation group, a respiratory virus from China, and power grid failures based on extreme weather. In mid-2020, when COVID-19 was picking up momentum, McGonigal received a call from a senior executive at World Bank who had participated in EVOKE and led one of the strategy teams ten years earlier and asked her, "How did you get so much right?"[12]

As it turns out, McGonigal spent an inordinate amount of time helping others imagine the future. Not so that any of them could necessarily get it all right or mitigate all risk but instead so they might develop new insight, balance worry with hope, and get very clear about what they could actually control. In a sense, her work was to help them forecast flux so that they could feel grounded in the midst of it.

Just like Sully, McGonigal knew the unexpected could come. So much so that she dedicated her work to helping others prepare for it. So, when one of her scenarios played out, she had already imagined making her way through it and helped others do the same.

Imagine a new global pandemic hit tomorrow. Yes, it would be disrupting, chaotic, and traumatic, but chances are we'd also feel like we had some mental frameworks and coping skills that we didn't have before 2020. This time, we'd have a set of skills we could integrate to help us navigate the disruption.

Preparation matters. Imagining tomorrow helps us today. Of course, most of us will never be able to forecast with the technical clarity of Jane McGonigal. Nor should we try. Most of us aren't wired that way. The goal of navigating life in flux isn't to predict what will happen with enough accuracy that we mitigate all our feelings of uncertainty. Rather, the goal is to develop counterintuitive skills and prepare ourselves in a way that breeds confidence, even hope. To be so attuned to God in moments of ambiguity that we shift from feeling anxious to anticipating what might come. Even if the wind roars or the fog rolls in, we have a kind of deep and lasting contentment that comes from God within.

As we arrange our lives to integrate and prepare in the various daily opportunities and interactions that present themselves, we can also practice contentment in a different way—namely, by engaging the spiritual practices that have been handed down for generations by people pursuing the way of Jesus. Because faith is fundamentally a communal endeavor, when we engage spiritual practices, we never do so alone. We connect with a movement of Christ that is sustaining and steady and, in turn, ground ourselves in an unstable world.

Practices are not just something we do. Practices do something *to* us. They form us. They shape our loves and longings.[13] In other words, we are calibrated toward what our actions have shaped us to love. Understanding this involves a complex reckoning with individual and corporate actions over the course of our human story, one in which we examine our own lives and are willing to wake up to that which is not of God that has shaped our longings.

For the Sake of Others

Our goal is to feel at home in flux. To be grounded amid disruption, whether it be the low hum of transition all around us or the acute pressure of a moment when everything feels upside down. But our goal has also never been just about us. The point of navigating our way home is never just so we can feel the steadiness of our own stability but instead so we can seek the best for others too.

We are implicated in rupture and repair, the ongoing movement of this world. We live in particular and peculiar times, and that means something. Flux is the context in which we breathe and eat, cry and laugh, grieve and hope. For love's sake, we're involved in it. My friend and celebrated author Steven Garber wrestles with it like this: "Why is it that we care? Why is it that we see ourselves implicated in the world, in the way the world is and isn't—and in that way it ought to be? And why does it seem that some do not care?"[14]

The more we wake up, let go, and set the compass that rearranges our lives, the more we grow accountable to our clearest sense of home—to the spaces made up of people who value us, love us, and hold us in holy and gracious ways. To these spaces and *from* these spaces, we owe something to our neighbors and the world. We owe our own affection and care, our honesty, vulnerability, and growth. We owe our advocacy and nurturing. We owe our commitment to act on that which is good and just and to truly seek the best for others in our spheres of influence. We owe our lives to the One who first calls us lovingly into being. We owe showing up as belongers wherever we are and in all the ways we put our hands, hearts, and heads to work in the world. Our lives matter, our presence matters, and we are implicated in all that God is lovingly up to in the world.

Elaine went on to have a celebrated career. In her prime, she was the CEO of a global billion-dollar company—the first female

CEO in her industry and at that level. In this role, Elaine succeeded a longtime leader who had a reputation for micromanaging. He decided to stay on as chairperson of the board even after his term as CEO was finished. Unfortunately, this chairperson created a difficult working environment for Elaine and others, but with the way things were structured, Elaine couldn't show him the door.

At one point, Elaine was negotiating an acquisition with another global billion-dollar company. Everyone knew that one of the two leadership teams would go shortly after the deal was completed. Because these decisions are always volatile at the highest levels, Elaine took hits at every step of the process. She believed the chairperson of her own company was so problematic that he needed to go, and that there was no way to get him out other than to volunteer for her leadership team to be the one to step aside.

The chairperson was finally out, but so was she.

She did it because she knew it was the right thing to do for the lives she was called to look out for. In this, and in so much else, Elaine was the teacher she always wanted to be, even as the personal cost, by all outward appearances, was very high. She modeled for her employees how to lead from a place of presence and calm, especially when things were at their toughest. She cared for them when their jobs were on the line. She did the right thing, even when it cost her.

In an age where we celebrate individual achievements and laud big accomplishments, it is an act of sheer resistance to steward any sense of power and privilege we have toward the needs of others. To declare that, as we grow in our capacity to tolerate and navigate the liminality of what used to be but is no longer and what might be but isn't quite yet, we do so with others in mind.

We do so for others. Not instead of for ourselves, but alongside.

Nearly fifty years after Roger and his friends made it home in the fog, Ocean Point experienced one of the foggiest and rainiest summers on record. The good boating days were few and far between. Roger's pride and joy, *The Point Taken*, stayed secured to its mooring in the cove day after day as he avidly scanned the weather reports for a glimpse of the sun.

One Friday morning the report looked hopeful, if a bit overcast. No fog or rain predicted. So off Roger went, with Lisa and two friends, to a favorite lunch spot, a thirty-minute boat ride away. As they ate their chowder and lobster rolls, the sun poked through and the clouds burned off to reveal a crisp blue sky. It was glorious.

After they left the restaurant and got back on their boat, they were planning where they wanted to go next, wanting to take full advantage of the sunny day. But as they edged closer to the open ocean, the wind shifted rapidly. Within three minutes they were fully engulfed in dense fog. Roger, five decades older now and with his GPS compass nearby, slowed the boat down a bit. He paused and strained to hear all the sounds around him. He calmly asked everyone else on the boat to listen as well and scan around them for other boats coming toward them, the biggest danger when the fog rolls in fast and thick.

He was very alert, but not at all anxious. He'd been here many times before.

The navigational equipment on the boat (far better than it was fifty years ago!) showed him exactly where the obstacles lay both below and on shore. Slowly, the bell buoys he was navigating toward came into view, one by one. That foghorn closest to home was audible and getting louder. But as he steered toward it, the navigational system revealed ledges and rocks dangerously close to the surface.

The only way forward was to turn away from the sounds of home and head back into the open ocean.

He had to go further into the fog.

Roger calmly asked everyone to be very still and absolutely quiet so that the boat stayed steady and there were no unexpected noises or movements to distract him as they headed out to open sea. He couldn't see more than an arm's length in front of himself, but he trusted he could make the whole trip that way. Not just for himself but for his friends.

As you cultivate and integrate these counterintuitive Navigational Skills, you will become perceptive to the world in new ways. You will notice things you never did before and let go of things you used to hold dear. For waking up begets waking up, and letting go begets letting go. Coming home to ourselves leads to, well, more coming home and slowly being at home in flux.

Blessed are the eyes that adjust to the fog.

Blessed are the ears that can decipher the bells.

Blessed are the hearts that orient toward the One who calls us home.

This is how we can stand confidently, knowing we can traverse a whole life in flux.

A Prayer for Being at Home in Flux

Lord,
help me to be present to this day,
attending to that which is mine to do
and never trying to be more generous than you.
Releasing anxiety,
resisting distraction
to move toward courage
and wisdom,
so that I might care deeply and act accordingly for the people
you bring to me today,
at home wherever I may be.

Amen.

ACKNOWLEDGMENTS

Michaela

Writing a book is hard, costly work. Gratefully, I have not "gone at it alone." Lisa, thanks for pitching that we do this book together. I am better for it.

Sometimes I joke that I have a sign on my head that says, "Tell me all your work crap." But I'm serious when I say thank you to all the people who've entrusted me with their toughest stories and their biggest hopes about work and leadership in an age of flux—be it during a cohort, a class, or over coffee. Whether at the airport, in my inbox, or even at the grocery store—your stories became the soundtrack in my head as I wrote this book. It is yours.

To the team at Baker Books, you are a joy to work with. Sara Shelton and Stephanie Duncan Smith—thank you for bringing your editorial gifts to bear on this work. It is better because of you. Wendy Wetzel and the entire Marketing/PR team, thank you for all you did to position this book well. And to all the folks behind the scenes, thank you. As always, it's a gift to work with Greg Johnson at WordServe Literary.

Special thanks to my team at the Max De Pree Center for Leadership at Fuller Seminary for the ways our collective work has helped to shape and sharpen my thinking in nearly every way—not to mention my own inner work. To Paul Matsushima, Mark Roberts, Meryl Herr, W. Ryan Guiterrez, Chelsea Logan, Jessica Fregoe, Raven Carey-James, Suzie Sang, Jennifer Woodruff Tait, and Abby Hoard, it's been great to team with you. And to the dozens of guides who have wholeheartedly led fifty-plus Road Ahead groups, your care for people in transition has been instructive for me in every way. Special thanks to Rebecca Johnson, Kathy Young, Terry Timm, Yolanda Miller, and Wayne Park.

To those who have advised this work and/or rooted for me professionally, formally or informally, I owe so much to you: Uli Chi, Jody Vanderwel, Mary Andringa, Tod Bolsinger, Beth Snyder, Jasmine Bellamy, Denise Daniels, Jimmy Lee, Lisa Slayton, Jeff Wright, Scott Cormode, Kara Powell, Roy Goble, Mark Roberts, Jessica Lewis, and my dad, Pat O'Donnell. Thank you.

To my dear friends Angela, Liz, Lyndsey, and Amy—thank you for believing in me and for welcoming me to believe in you. We've endured so much of life in flux together. You've been the safest of spaces to name my greatest hopes and fears in all this. I hope I've been the same for you. And to the Phoebes: thank you for your deep well of love and friendship.

Thanks to my mother, Maureen O'Donnell, a therapist for thirty-plus years, for giving this book your stamp of approval. And lastly, thanks to my husband, Daniel Long, who not only tolerates but embraces my verbal processing way of existing and graciously listened and gave feedback to every little idea along the way.

I am so grateful for my trusted crew.

Lisa

My journey into this work began nearly thirty years ago as I faced a bombardment of life crises. The death of my father, the illness of my mother, and the adoption of my newborn child were the big ones. These disorienting and disruptive experiences sent me into a deep existential search for meaning in my own life but also in the world. My life was in flux.

Early in my journey, I met Richard M. Wellock, whose influence on who I am, and how I think and bring myself to this work, has been profound. Rick invited me into his world, a universe of its own in many ways. He taught me the power of good questions and how to listen deeply. He remains my very own Yoda. He is my brother in Christ, and I love him deeply.

I entered the world of Leadership Foundations in the early 2000s, and this crazy bunch of Jesus lovers have become my brothers and sisters on this journey. I am grateful to John Stahl-Wert for inviting me in. These are men and women who care about the most vulnerable and are committed to their cities becoming more like playgrounds than battlegrounds. It was here that I designed a six-month cohort program that served over four hundred leaders over twelve years in navigating various seasons of life in flux.

Dr. Brad Smith and Bakke Graduate University shaped me through a master's program that expanded my world and worldview. The influence of R. Paul Stevens, John Lewis, H. Spees, and the international faculty of BGU further built a solid theological base for my practical work in the world. The questions and teaching of Tim Keller, Steve Garber, H. Spees, and R. Paul Stevens have helped me frame and shape my work in the world.

Katherine Leary Alsdorf, who founded and led the Center for Faith and Work at Redeemer Church, offered a vision for redemptive work in every sphere of influence that was integral to my own, as I increasingly worked with business leaders and entrepreneurs.

My team at Pittsburgh Leadership Foundation was the very best, and it was a joy to work with Jim Stout, Mike McGreevy, Jay Slocum, Katie Tarara, Terry Timm, Katie Wentz, Herb Kolbe, and Emily Jensen as we endeavored to bring the vision of PLF to life in our precious city.

I am grateful for the friendship of women who have come in the form of a monthly prayer group called the Phoebes. Thank you to Denise Daniels, Stephanie Summers, Joanna Meyer, Kara Martin, Missy Wallace, and my beloved coauthor, Michaela O'Donnell. I love you all and am grateful for your support and encouragement.

To the many people I have walked with through the flux in their own lives, I am forever grateful for your trust. Your stories inhabit these pages in form and function, bits of your journey shared here to help others in the fog.

The community of Ocean Point, Maine, has been a part of most of my adult life. Roger Slayton brought me here in 1980, and we have been going back every summer since. It is, more than any other place I have lived, home.

I am grateful for my dear child, now an adult, Rain, who has taught me more than anyone about patience and compassion.

Roger is steadfast and strong, and a wise captain in the foggiest of moments. I love him with my whole heart. And there is no one whom I trust more to navigate through the fog with, real and metaphorical. I am blessed beyond measure every day.

NOTES

Chapter 1 Life in Flux

1. This definition is a nod to William Bridges's seminal work *Transitions*. He describes the patterns of experiences for a class he taught: "As we listed them on the board the first night, the three main similarities seemed to be what we all had experienced: (1) an ending, followed by (2) a period of confusion and distress, leading to (3) a new beginning, for those who had come that far." William Bridges with Susan Bridges, *Transitions: Making Sense of Life's Changes*, fortieth anniversary ed. (New York: Hachette, 2019), 8.

2. Bruce Feiler, *Life Is in the Transitions: Mastering Change at Any Age* (New York: Penguin, 2020), 16. See also Arthur C. Brooks, "The Clocklike Regularity of Major Life Changes," *Atlantic*, September 10, 2020, https://www.theatlantic.com/family/archive/2020/09/major-life-changes-happen-clocklike-regularity/616243/.

3. Feiler, *Life Is in the Transitions*, 79.

4. Feiler, *Life Is in the Transitions*, 79.

5. Peter Senge's work is seminal for thinking about how one part of a system impacts another. See Peter Senge, *The Fifth Discipline: The Art & Practice of the Learning Organization*, rev. and updated ed. (New York: Doubleday, 2006).

6. Futurist Ray Kurzweil suggests that the rate of change in the twenty-first century will be nearly twenty thousand times what it was in the twentieth century, stating that change, especially technological change, is exponential, not linear. See Ray Kurzweil, *The Singularity Is Near: When Humans Transcend Biology* (New York: Penguin, 2006), 12.

7. Thomas Friedman, *Thank You for Being Late: An Optimist's Guide to Thriving in the Age of Accelerations* (New York: Farrar, Straus & Giroux, 2016), 29.

8. Friedman, *Thank You for Being Late*, 29.

9. Friedman, *Thank You for Being Late*, 29–30.

10. Daniel J. Levitin, "Why the Modern World Is Bad for Your Brain," *The Guardian*, January 18, 2015, https://www.theguardian.com/science/2015/jan/18/modern-world-bad-for-brain-daniel-j-levitin-organized-mind-information-overload.

11. For more on this story, see Michaela O'Donnell, *Make Work Matter: Your Guide to Meaningful Work in a Changing World* (Grand Rapids: Baker Books, 2021).

12. Author William Bridges describes, "When you're in transition, you find yourself coming back in new ways to old activities." Bridges, *Transitions*, 7.

13. At the time of publishing, we have run nearly sixty Road Ahead cohorts for people asking vocational questions in seasons of transition. Though the curriculum is rooted in my dissertation research, the cohort is a team effort in every way.

14. In his foreword to Alex Pattakos's *Prisoners of Our Thoughts*, Stephen Covey describes reading a quote that made him think of Austrian psychiatrist and Holocaust survivor Viktor Frankl's work. The quote has since been attributed to Frankl even though he's not the original source. See Alex Pattakos, *Prisoners of Our Thoughts: Viktor Frankl's Principles for Discovering Meaning in Life and Work*, third ed. (Oakland: Berrett-Koehler, 2017), vi.

15. Though there are many different definitions of anxiety and stress and how the two are related, Lisa and I have chosen to use the American Psychological Association's description of how the two are different. See Mary Alvord and Raquel Halfond, "What's the Difference between Stress and Anxiety," American Psychological Association, October 28, 2019, https://www.apa.org/topics/stress/anxiety-difference.

16. Alvord and Halfond, "What's the Difference Between Stress and Anxiety."

17. Joanna Cheek, "Stress First Aid as a Form of Peer Support," This Changed My Practice (UBC CPD), August 5, 2020, https://thischangedmypractice.com/stress-first-aid-as-a-form-of-peer-support/.

18. David Whyte, *Consolations: The Solace, Nourishment and Underlying Meaning of Everyday Words* (Langley, WA: Many Rivers Press, 2015), 49–51.

19. "I hereby command you: Be strong and courageous; do not be frightened or dismayed, for the LORD your God is with you wherever you go" (Josh. 1:9 NRSVUE).

20. Uli Chi, *The Wise Leader* (Grand Rapids: Eerdmans, 2024), 2–4.

21. Richard Rohr talks about going down to go up as a "spirituality of imperfection." See Richard Rohr, *Falling Upward: A Spirituality for the Two Halves of Life* (San Francisco: Jossey-Bass, 2011), Kindle loc. 356.

22. "*Metamorphosis*: Film Clips," Illustra Media, accessed December 20, 2023, http://www.metamorphosisthefilm.com/clips.php.

23. See 2 Corinthians 5:16.

24. Henri J. M. Nouwen, *In the Name of Jesus: Reflections on Christian Leadership* (New York: Crossroads, 1989), 22.

25. Nouwen, *In the Name of Jesus*, 22.

Chapter 2 Prepare to Wake Up

1. Miriam Greenspan, *Healing through the Dark Emotions: The Wisdom of Grief, Fear, and Despair* (Boston: Shambhala, 2004), Kindle loc. 235–43.

2. Bono, *Surrender: 40 Songs, One Story* (New York: Knopf, 2022), 214.

3. Henri Nouwen, *Following Jesus: Finding Our Way Home in an Age of Anxiety* (New York: Convergent, 2019), 21.

4. Thanks to Jennifer Guerra Aldana for teaching me to pray this psalm, in this translation, so many years ago. It is stamped on my heart forever.

5. The exercise also appeared in my first book, *Make Work Matter*.

6. Susan Cain, *Bittersweet: How Sorrow and Longing Make Us Whole* (New York: Crown, 2022), Kindle loc. xxvi.

Chapter 3 Check Your Speed

1. Kevin P. Madore and Anthony D. Wagner, "Multicosts of Multitasking," *Cerebrum*, March–April 2019, https://www.ncbi.nlm.nih.gov/pmc/articles/PMC7075496/.

2. Kim Parker, "About a Third of U.S. Workers Who Can Work From Home Now Do So All the Time," Pew Research Center, March 30, 2023, https://www.pewresearch.org/short-reads/2023/03/30/about-a-third-of-us-workers-who-can-work-from-home-do-so-all-the-time/.

3. Microsoft Worklab, "Research Proves Your Brain Needs Breaks," Microsoft, April 20, 2021, https://www.microsoft.com/en-us/worklab/work-trend-index/brain-research.

4. American Psychological Association, "Multitasking: Switching Costs," American Psychological Association, March 20, 2006, https://www.apa.org/topics/research/multitasking.

5. Oliver Burkeman, "Escaping the Efficiency Trap—and Finding Some Peace of Mind," *Wall Street Journal*, August 6, 2021, https://www.wsj.com/articles/escaping-the-efficiency-trapand-finding-some-peace-of-mind-11628262751.

6. Burkeman, "Escaping the Efficiency Trap."

7. This phrasing is a nod to the movie *Everything Everywhere All at Once*, the 2022 sensation written and directed by Daniel Kwan and Daniel Scheinert and starring Michelle Yeoh, Stephanie Hsu, and Jamie Lee Curtis.

8. Bessel van der Kolk, *The Body Keeps the Score: Brain, Mind, and Body in the Healing of Trauma* (New York: Penguin, 2015), 70–71.

9. This next section is adapted from an article I wrote for Fuller Studio: Michaela O'Donnell, "Reassessing Our Relationship with Work and Rest," *Fuller Magazine* 22, February 15, 2022, https://fullerstudio.fuller.edu/theology/reassessing-our-relationship-with-work-and-rest/.

10. Derek Thompson, "Workism Is Making Americans Miserable," *Atlantic*, February 24, 2019, https://www.theatlantic.com/ideas/archive/2019/02/religion-workism-making-americans-miserable/583441/.

11. Jonathan Malesic, "The Future of Work Should Mean Working Less," *New York Times*, September 23, 2021, https://www.nytimes.com/interactive/2021/09/23/opinion/covid-return-to-work-rto.html.

12. Aaron De Smet, Bonnie Dowling, Marino Mugayar-Baldocchi, and Bill Schaninger, "'Great Attrition' or 'Great Attraction'? The Choice Is Yours," *McKinsey Quarterly*, September 8, 2021, https://www.mckinsey.com/capabilities/people-and-organizational-performance/our-insights/great-attrition-or-great-attraction-the-choice-is-yours.

13. Jim Harter, "Is Quiet Quitting Real?," Gallup, September 6, 2022, https://www.gallup.com/workplace/398306/quiet-quitting-real.aspx.

14. U.S. Bureau of Labor Statistics, "Average Hours Per Day Spent in Selected Activities on Days Worked by Employment Status and Sex," Bureau of Labor Statistics Graphics for Economics News Releases, accessed December 20, 2023, https://www.bls.gov/charts/american-time-use/activity-by-work.htm.

15. U.S. Travel Association, "Study: A Record 768 Million U.S. Vacation Days Went Unused in '18, Opportunity Cost in the Billions," U.S. Travel Association, August 16, 2019, https://www.ustravel.org/press/study-record-768-million-us-vacation-days-went-unused-18-opportunity-cost-billions.

16. Erik Sherman, "49% of Americans Under 35 Report Having a 'Side Hustle,'" *Fortune*, June 6, 2019, https://fortune.com/2019/06/06/gig-economy-part-time-jobs/. See also Juliana Menasce Horowitz and Kim Parker, "How Americans View Their Jobs," Pew Research Center, March 30, 2023, https://www.pewresearch.org/social-trends/2023/03/30/how-americans-view-their-jobs/.

17. This language and concept of Sabbath as resistance comes from Walter Brueggemann, *Sabbath as Resistance: Saying No to a Culture of Now* (Louisville: John Knox, 2014).

18. Center for Action and Contemplation, "What Is Contemplation?" Center for Action and Contemplation, accessed December 4, 2023, https://cac.org/about/what-is-contemplation/.

19. Barbara Peacock, *Soul Care in African American Practice* (Downers Grove, IL: InterVarsity, 2020), 55.

20. Peacock, *Soul Care*, 54. See also Rosa Parks and Gregory J. Reed, *Quiet Strength: The Faith, the Hope, and the Heart of a Woman Who Changed a Nation* (Grand Rapids: Zondervan, 1994).

21. Center for Action and Contemplation, "What Is Contemplation: Practice-Based Spirituality," Center for Action and Contemplation, accessed December 4, 2023, https://cac.org/about/what-is-contemplation/#:~:text=Practice%2DBased%20Spirituality,ecstatic%20singing%2C%20or%20chanting.

22. O'Donnell, *Make Work Matter*, 210.

Chapter 4 Choose to Let Go

1. I first told my letting go story in my book *Make Work Matter*, but because this skill is one I'm still mastering, it's worth narrating again here.

2. Adapted from Lisa Pratt Slayton's "Leading from Betwixt and Between," Tamim Partners, April 29, 2020, https://tamimpartners.com/the-big-quit-1/part4/wordlewithfriends/1/sphfa6mnm3ysgbwdf3ngxpsaze2nze.

3. William Bridges says, "Rule number one: when you're in transition, you find yourself coming back in new ways to old activities." Bridges, *Transitions*, 7.

4. Henry Cloud, *Necessary Endings: The Employees, Businesses, and Relationships That All of Us Have to Give Up in Order to Move Forward* (New York: Harper Business, 2011), 6.

5. David G. Benner, *Surrender to Love: Discovering the Heart of Christian Spirituality* (Downers Grove, IL: InterVarsity), 41–42.

6. "There is no fear in love, but perfect love casts out fear; for fear has to do with punishment, and whoever fears has not reached perfection in love" (1 John 4:18 NRSVUE).

7. Ronald A. Heifetz and Marty Linsky, *Leadership on the Line: Staying Alive through the Dangers of Leadership* (Boston: Harvard Business Review, 2022).

8. Stephen R. Covey, *The 7 Habits of Highly Effective People*, thirtieth anniversary ed. (New York: Simon & Schuster, 2020). When I googled "Circle of Control," I got over four billion hits as of December 2023.

9. These questions were originally developed by Lisa Slayton for use in Tamim Partners, LLC's executive coaching and organizational development practice.

10. Daniel Goleman, "What Makes a Leader?," *Harvard Business Review*, January 2004, https://hbr.org/2004/01/what-makes-a-leader.

11. Greenspan, *Healing through the Dark Emotions*, Kindle loc. 169.

12. Greenspan, *Healing through the Dark Emotions*, Kindle loc. 176.

13. Elisabeth Kübler-Ross, *On Death and Dying: What the Dying Have to Teach Doctors, Nurses, Clergy, and their Own Families*, fiftieth anniversary ed. (New York: Scribner, 2014).

14. Patrick Tyrrell, Seneca Harberger, Caroline Schoo, and Waquar Siddiqui, "Kubler-Ross Stages of Dying and Subsequent Models of Grief," StatPearls, updated February 26, 2023, https://www.ncbi.nlm.nih.gov/books/NBK507885/.

15. Meg Bernhard, "What If There's No Such Thing as Closure?," *New York Times*, December 15, 2021, https://www.nytimes.com/2021/12/15/magazine/grieving-loss-closure.html.

16. Bernhard, "What If There's No Such Thing as Closure?"

17. This paragraph and the next are adapted from O'Donnell, *Make Work Matter*, 152–53.

18. See "Healthy Marketplace Leaders Research," Max De Pree Center for Leadership, accessed December 20, 2023, https://depree.org/research/marketplace/.

Chapter 5 Embrace the Unfiguroutable

1. "Most of us take pride in our knowledge and expertise, and in staying true to our beliefs and opinions. That makes sense in a stable world, where we get rewarded for having conviction in our ideas. The problem is that we live in a rapidly changing world, where we need to spend as much time rethinking as we do thinking." Adam Grant, *Think Again: The Power of Knowing What You Don't Know* (New York: Viking, 2021), 16.

2. Jack Mezirow, *Transformative Dimensions of Adult Learning* (San Francisco: Jossey-Bass, 1991), Kindle loc. 99.

3. Richard Rohr, "Introduction," in *Oneing: An Alternative Orthodoxy: Liminal Space* 8, no. 1 (January 2020): 17–20.

4. Mezirow, *Transformative Dimensions of Adult Learning*.

5. Rohr, *Falling Upward*, 127–36.

6. Grant, *Think Again*, 2.

7. Alison Cook, *The Best of You: Break Free from Painful Patterns, Mend Your Past, and Discover Your True Self in God* (Nashville: Thomas Nelson, 2022), 44.

8. Cook, *Best of You*, 45, 218.

9. I'm indebted to the practical theologians whose work has informed mine. A couple of books that have been particularly formative for me are: Mark Lau Branson and Juan F. Martínex, *Churches, Cultures, and Leadership: A Practical Theology of Congregations and Ethnicities* (Downers Grove, IL: InterVarsity, 2011), and Richard Osmer, *Practical Theology: An Introduction* (Grand Rapids: Eerdmans, 2008).

10. Mezirow, *Transformative Dimensions of Adult Learning*, Kindle loc. 212.

11. Heifetz and Linsky, *Leadership on the Line*.

Chapter 6 Set Your Compass

1. O'Donnell, *Make Work Matter*, 65–90.

2. Mark D. Roberts, "God's Transformational Calling, Part 2: Calling from a Caller," Max De Pree Center for Leadership, accessed December 28, 2023, https://depree.org/series/gods-transformational-calling/#part2.

3. See 1 Corinthians 1:1.

4. Henry Cloud and John Townsend, *How People Grow: What the Bible Reveals about Personal Growth* (Grand Rapids: Zondervan, 2004), 117.

5. O'Donnell, *Make Work Matter*, 65–90.

6. Patrick B. Reyes, *Nobody Cries When We Die: God, Community, and Surviving to Adulthood* (Des Peres, MO: Chalice Press, 2016); Patrick B. Reyes, *The Purpose Gap: Empowering Communities of Color to Find Meaning and Thrive* (Louisville: Westminster John Knox, 2021); Steven Garber, The *Seamless Life: A Tapestry of Love & Learning, Worship & Work* (Downers Grove, IL: InterVarsity, 2020).

7. Reyes, *The Purpose Gap*, 34.

8. Ruth Haley Barton, "Discernment: The Heart of Spiritual Leadership," Transforming Center, accessed December 6, 2023, https://transformingcenter.org/2012/05/discernment-the-heart-of-spiritual-leadership/.

Chapter 7 Come Home to Yourself

1. Thomas Merton, *New Seeds of Contemplation* (repr. New York: New Directions, 2007), 37.

2. The tagline for Suzanne and Joe Stabile's Life in the Trinity Ministry is "A place for solitary work that cannot be done alone." See https://www.lifeinthetrinityministry.com/home.

3. Patrick Reyes, "Michaela O'Donnell: Context and Constraints: Integrating Life, Work, and Faith," *Sound of the Genuine* (podcast), March 8, 2023, https://podcasts.apple.com/us/podcast/michaela-odonnell-contexts-and-constraints/id1572223219?i=1000603646826.

4. Greenspan, *Healing through the Dark Emotions*, Kindle loc. 58–63.

5. Greenspan, *Healing through the Dark Emotions*, Kindle loc. 58–63.

6. Edwin H. Friedman, *A Failure of Nerve: Leadership in the Age of the Quick Fix* (New York: Church Publishing, 2017).

7. Cook, *The Best of You*, 11.

8. Tim Keller wrote, "Because He loves me and He accepts me, I do not have to do things just to build up my résumé. I do not have to do things to make me look good. I can do things for the joy of doing them. I can help people to help people—not so I can feel better about myself, not so I can fill up the emptiness."

Timothy Keller, *The Freedom of Self-Forgetfulness: The Path to True Christian Joy* (Louisville: 10 Publishing, 2021), 15.

9. Rohr, *Falling Upward*, 130.

10. Beatrice Chestnut, *The Complete Enneagram: 27 Paths to Greater Self-Knowledge* (Berkeley, CA: She Writes Press, 2013).

11. In her coaching work with people, Lisa has long used a very helpful process called the System for Identifying Motivated Abilities® (SIMA).

12. Teresa M. Amabile, "How to Kill Creativity," *Harvard Business Review*, September–October 1998, 78–79, https://hbr.org/1998/09/how-to-kill-creativity.

13. SIMA is built on a core foundation that each of us is unique and that our own stories can illuminate how we are moving when we are working at our best.

14. Artsper, "Kintsugi, or the Japanese Art of Mending Ceramics with Gold," *Artsper Magazine*, December 27, 2021, https://blog.artsper.com/en/lifestyle/the -kintsugi-or-the-japanese-art-of-mending-ceramics-with-gold/.

15. "Kintsugi, Mended with Gold Reflection," video, 3:53, Windrider Studios, https://www.windriderstudios.org/kintsugi-collection/videos/kintsugi-mended -with-gold-reflection.

16. "Kintsugi, The W," video, 6:13, Windrider Studios, https://www.windrider studios.org/kintsugi-collection/videos/kintsugi-the-w.

17. "Kintsugi, Mended with Gold Reflection."

Chapter 8 Don't Go It Alone

1. Vivek H. Murthy, "Our Epidemic of Loneliness and Isolation: The U.S. Surgeon General's Advisory on the Healing Effects of Social Connection and Community," Office of the Surgeon General, 2023, pdf loc. 7, https://www.hhs .gov/sites/default/files/surgeon-general-social-connection-advisory.pdf.

2. Susie Demarinis, "Loneliness at Epidemic Levels in America," *Explore* (NY) 16, no. 5 (September–October 2020): 278–79, https://www.ncbi.nlm.nih.gov/pmc /articles/PMC7321652/.

3. Demarinis, "Loneliness at Epidemic Levels in America."

4. Centers for Disease Control and Prevention, "Loneliness and Social Isolation Linked to Serious Health Conditions," CDC Alzheimer's Disease and Healthy Aging Program, accessed December 28, 2023, https://www.cdc.gov/aging /publications/features/lonely-older-adults.html.

5. Murthy, "Our Epidemic of Loneliness and Isolation," 4.

6. Robert Waldinger and Marc Schulz, *The Good Life: Lessons from the World's Longest Scientific Study of Happiness* (New York: Simon & Schuster, 2023), 29.

7. Waldinger and Schulz, *The Good Life*, 29.

8. Tish Harrison Warren, "What If Burnout Is Less about Work and More about Isolation?," *New York Times*, October 9, 2022, https://www.nytimes.com /2022/10/09/opinion/burnout-friends-isolation.html.

9. Tish Harrison Warren, "We're in a Loneliness Crisis: Another Reason to Get Off Our Phones," *New York Times*, May 1, 2022, https://www.nytimes.com /2022/05/01/opinion/loneliness-connectedness-technology.html.

10. Murthy, "Our Epidemic of Loneliness and Isolation," 11.

11. Stanley J. Grenz and Jay T. Smith, *Created for Community: Connecting Christian Belief with Christian Living* (Grand Rapids: Baker, 1996), 15–16.

12. See Isaiah 49:15 and Hosea 13:8.

13. Jürgen Moltmann, *The Trinity and the Kingdom* (Minneapolis: Fortress, 1993), Kindle loc. 443.

14. Grenz and Smith, *Created for Community*, 18.

15. As quoted in Grenz and Smith, *Created for Community*, 18.

16. Grenz and Smith, *Created for Community*, 50.

17. Grenz and Smith, *Created for Community*, 51.

18. M. Maegele et al., "The 2004 Tsunami Disaster: Injury Pattern and Microbiological Aspects," *Critical Care* 10, suppl. 1 (March 21, 2006): 128, https://www.ncbi.nlm.nih.gov/pmc/articles/PMC4092503/.

19. STAR is a collaborative project involving investigators at Duke University, the University of North Carolina at Chapel Hill, SurveyMETER (Indonesia), the University of California, Los Angeles (UCLA), the University of Pennsylvania, the University of Southern California, the World Bank, and Statistics Indonesia. For more information, see "The STAR Project," STAR: Study of Tsunami Aftermath and Recovery, http://stardata.org/index.html.

20. Mary-Russell Roberson, "After the Tsunami: 10 Years of Recovery and Resilience," *Stanford Insights*, Fall 2014, 8–10, http://stardata.org/Research/14Fall _Insights.pdf.

21. Bernard of Clairvaux, *Sermons on the Song of Songs: Medieval Theology* (San Francisco: Fig, 2013), Kindle loc. 99.

22. Patrick B. Reyes and Lisa Slayton, "The Big Quit: A Crisis of Calling," video, 58:26, CityGate Labs, March 17, 2022, https://citygate.com/monthly-labs /calling-and-context.

23. Grenz and Smith, *Created for Community*, 40.

24. Wendell Berry, *Jayber Crow: A Novel* (Berkeley: Counterpoint, 2000), 338.

25. Warren, "What If Burnout Is Less about Work?"

26. Ben Cohen, "A Psychologist Spent Five Years Studying World Cup Penalty Shootouts," *Wall Street Journal*, December 9, 2022, https://www.wsj.com/articles /world-cup-penalty-kick-shootout-geir-jordet-11670449695.

27. Adapted from Michaela O'Donnell, "The Benefit (and Risk) of Leading with Care," *De Pree Journal*, January 19, 2023, https://depree.org/the-benefit-and -risk-of-leading-with-care/.

Chapter 9 Stay in Your Headlights

1. George Plimpton, "E. L. Doctorow, The Art of Fiction No. 94," *The Paris Review* 101, Winter 1986, https://www.theparisreview.org/interviews/2718/the -art-of-fiction-no-94-e-l-doctorow.

2. If we're not careful, this might sound like we're advocating for a kind of passivity that's at the heart of so much of what's wrong in the world. We are not advocating tossing our hands in the air at the world's problems. On the contrary, we're advocating for a clear sense of what is ours to do as we participate in the work of God in the world.

3. Brené Brown, "Emily Nagoski and Amelia Nagoski on Burnout and How to Complete the Stress Cycle," *Unlocking Us with Brené Brown*, October 14, 2020, https://brenebrown.com/podcast/brene-with-emily-and-amelia-nagoski-on -burnout-and-how-to-complete-the-stress-cycle/#transcript.

4. Parker Palmer, *Let Your Life Speak: Listening for the Voice of Vocation* (San Francisco: Jossey-Bass, 2000), Kindle loc. 476.

5. Byung-Chul Han, *The Burnout Society* (Stanford: Stanford University Press, 2010), 4.

6. Brené Brown, *Dare to Lead: Brave Work, Tough Conversations, Whole Hearts* (New York: Random House, 2018), 20.

7. Susan Maros, *Calling in Context: Social Location and Vocational Formation* (Downers Grove, IL: InterVarsity, 2022), 13–27.

Chapter 10 At Home in Flux

1. Bridges, *Transitions*, 27.

2. Philosopher Friedrich Nietzsche is quoted, "The essential thing 'in heaven and earth' is . . . that there should be long obedience in the same direction; there thereby results, and has always resulted in the long run, something which has made life worth living." Friedrich Nietzsche, *Beyond Good and Evil*, trans. Helen Zimmern (Berwyn Heights, MD: Heritage Books, 2014), 51.

3. Bridges, *Transitions*, 78.

4. Dan B. Allender, *To Be Told: God Invites You to Coauthor Your Future* (Colorado Springs: WaterBrook, 2006), 103.

5. Dallas Willard, *The Spirit of the Disciplines: Understanding How God Changes Lives* (repr., New York: HarperOne, 1999), Kindle loc. xx.

6. P. A. Geddie, "Taking the High Road with Sully," *County Line Magazine*, December 29, 2020, https://www.countylinemagazine.com/life-style/taking -the-high-road-with-sully/article_5c764e58-4478-11eb-bfd6-17790552bcda.html.

7. The phrase "entrusted to their care" is from Scott Cormode. I find it a helpful reframe on the task of leadership. For his thinking on the topic, see Scott Cormode, "A People Entrusted to Your Care," Fuller Studio, accessed December 28, 2023, https://fullerstudio.fuller.edu/a-people-entrusted-to-your-care/.

8. Willard, *Spirit of the Disciplines*, Kindle loc. 4.

9. Willard, *Spirit of the Disciplines*, Kindle loc. 4.

10. Jane McGonigal, *Imaginable: How to See the Future Coming and Feel Ready for Anything—Even Things That Seem Impossible Today* (New York: Spiegel & Grau, 2022), 8–28.

11. McGonigal, *Imaginable*, xix.

12. McGonigal, *Imaginable*, xx.

13. See Dorothy Bass, ed., *Practicing Our Faith*, second ed. (San Francisco: Jossey-Bass, 2010), 7–10; James K. A. Smith, *You Are What You Love: The Spiritual Power of Habit* (Grand Rapids: Brazos, 2016); Craig Dykstra, *Growing in the Life of Faith: Education and Christian Practices*, second ed. (Louisville: Westminster John Knox, 2005), 56. Craig Dykstra's definition of practice: "those cooperative human activities through which we, as individuals and as communities, grow and develop in moral character and substance" (*Growing in the Life of Faith*, 69). Dykstra's definition is built partly on Alasdair MacIntyre's seminal work on practices, *After Virtue*, in that it defines practice as a cooperative, human, and social established reality.

14. Steven Garber, *Visions of Vocation: Common Grace for the Common Good* (Downers Grove, IL: InterVarsity, 2014), Kindle loc. 116.

Michaela O'Donnell, PhD, is executive director of Fuller Seminary's Max De Pree Center for Leadership. The author of *Make Work Matter*, Michaela is a sought-after speaker and consultant who regularly presents on the topics of vocation, career, and leadership to religious, secular, academic, and lay audiences.

CONNECT WITH MICHAELA

LinkedIn.com/in/Michaela-O-Donnell/

@Michaela.Odonnell

Lisa Pratt Slayton is the founding partner and CEO of Tamim Partners, LLC, providing coaching and consulting to executives, businesses, nonprofits, and churches. She also serves as a board director for the Leadership Foundations network.

CONNECT WITH LISA

TamimPartners.com

LinkedIn.com/in/Lisa-Slayton-015aa01/

@LobsterLisa